AUTHORS ACKNOWLEDGE

First and foremost, I would like to extend my deepest gratitude to the mentors, financial experts, and educators who have tirelessly shared their knowledge and insights, inspiring individuals to engage with the financial markets at every stage of life.

Their dedication to financial literacy has been instrumental in shaping the foundation of this work.

And the TRADING AS A SUBJECT COMMUNITY for the extended research and providing the right knowledge to their students and community and for staying committed to teaching people about the Financial Markets and how to approach and Trade them

Adulthood and Financial Stability

Peak Phase and Legacy Planning
The journey of engaging with financial markets from a young age through to adulthood is a transformative one
It is my sincere hope that this work inspires individuals to embrace financial literacy and market participation as a lifelong endeavour.

booksasasubject.store

TABLE OF CONTENTS

1. BASIC KNOWLEDGE OF THE FINANCIAL MARKET — [3](#)
2. THE DIGITAL WORLD WE LIVE IN — [7](#)
3. THE CURRENT STATE OF THE WORLD FINANCIAL WISE — [15](#)
5. RELATIONSHIP BETWEEN TECHNOLOGY AND FINANCIAL MARKETS — [15](#)
6. FINANCIAL MARKET IMPACT ON OUR EVERYDAY LIVES — [17](#)
[17](#) TENDER AGE (CHILDHOOD TO TEENAGE YEARS) — [17](#)

booksasasubject.store

6.1	**FINANCIAL LITERACY**	**17**
6.2	**CRITICAL THINKING AND PROBLEM-SOLVING**	**18**
6.3	**RESPONSIBILITY AND DISCIPLINE**	**19**
6.4	**FUTURE PREPAREDNESS**	**20**
7.	YOUTH (20S TO EARLY 30S)	**25**
7.1	TIME ADVANTAGE	**26**
7.2	**RISK TOLERANCE**	**27**
7.3	**FINANCIAL INDEPENDENCE**	**28**
7.4	SKILL DEVELOPMENT	**29**

8.	**ADULTHOOD (30S TO EARLY 50S)**	**32**
8.1	WEALTH ACCUMULATION	32
8.2	RETIREMENT PLANNING	33
8.3	FINANCIAL GOALS	34
8.4	INFLATION PROTECTION	35
9.	PEAK ADULT PHASE (50S AND BEYOND)	46
9.1	**WEALTH PRESERVATION**	46
9.2	**LEGACY BUILDING**	47

9.3		CONTINUED ENGAGEMENT	<u>48</u>
9.4		SUPPORT FOR LIFESTYLE	<u>49</u>
10.		STARTING YOUNG: THE TENDER AGE	<u>50</u>
11.		TEENAGE YEARS AND EARLY YOUTH	<u>51</u>
12.		ENTERING ADULTHOOD	<u>52</u>
13.		PEAK ADULT PHASE	<u>53</u>
14.		THE BENEFITS OF EARLY FINANCIAL INVOLVEMENT	<u>56</u>
15.		CASE STUDIES AND REAL-LIFE EXAMPLES	<u>63</u>

PREFACE

The motivation behind this e-book is to demystify the financial markets and empower readers with the knowledge needed to navigate them confidently. Whether you're a beginner looking to make informed investment decisions or someone seeking to deepen your understanding, this book aims to provide clarity and insight.

exploring key concepts and practical strategies, I hope to inspire a new level of awareness and engagement with financial markets. My goal is to equip you with the tools to make sound financial choices and to foster a sense of empowerment in managing your financial future

Thank you for embarking on this journey with me.

In today's world, financial markets are integral to our daily lives, yet they remain a mystery to many. Despite their impact on our economies and personal finances, a significant portion of the population does not understand how these markets operate. This knowledge gap can lead to missed opportunities and financial missteps.

DISCLAIMER

The information provided in this ebook is for educational and informational purposes only. It is not intended to be and does not constitute financial advice, investment advice, trading advice, or any other advice. You should not make any financial decision based on the information provided in this e-book without consulting a qualified financial advisor. The author of this e-book is not a licensed financial advisor. The content of this e-book reflects the author's opinions and perspectives and should not be construed as professional financial advice. Trading and investing in financial markets involves risk. Past performance is not necessarily indicative of future results. The author assumes no responsibility for any losses or damages that may result from the use of information contained in this e-book.

booksasasubject.store

INTRODUCTION

As a young man who is in his early 30's I wish I knew earlier in my teenage years about the Financial Markets and how it operates not to mentions its pros I would have a better understanding of money and how it operates . Wealth would have been the topic of the day and with those who follow after me I am still glad that I got a chance to learn about it even at this stage of my life because it really does not matter where in the world you are and who you are and what stage of life you are in at the moment. Just take this opportunity and embark on a journey of learning about the Financial Markets . Ladies and Gentleman please sit down relax your mind and take a voyage to learning how to bring about Financial freedom into your life. Because this might just be the most exciting and beneficial experience that you have ever encounter so far in your entire existence , if you had one , well , lets take this opportunity and add onto your arsenal.

booksasasubject.store

Financial markets are platforms or systems that facilitate the buying, selling, and trading of financial assets such as stocks, bonds, commodities, and currencies. These markets play a crucial role in the global economy by providing a mechanism for allocating resources, determining prices, and enabling companies and governments to raise capital.

Types of Financial Markets

Stock markets

Primary Market

Where new securities are issued and sold to investors for the first time. Companies use this market to raise capital by issuing shares during an Initial Public Offering (IPO).

Secondary Market:

Where existing securities are traded among investors. The New York Stock Exchange (NYSE) and NASDAQ are examples of secondary markets.

Bond Markets

These markets deal with the issuance and trading of debt securities. Governments and corporations issue bonds to raise funds, and investors buy these bonds to receive periodic interest payments and the return of principal upon maturity.

Commodity Markets

These markets involve the trading of physical goods such as gold, oil, and agricultural products. Commodities can be traded on spot markets for immediate delivery or on futures markets for delivery at a later date.

Foreign Exchange Markets (Forex)

The forex market is where currencies are traded. It is the largest and most liquid financial market in the world. Participants include governments, banks, corporations, and individual traders.

Derivatives Markets

These markets trade financial instruments such as futures, options, and swaps, which derive their value from underlying assets like stocks, bonds, or commodities.

Money Markets

These markets deal with short-term debt instruments and are used by participants to manage their liquidity needs. Examples include Treasury bills and commercial paper.

Key Functions of Financial Markets

Price Discovery
Financial markets help in determining the prices of financial instruments through supply and demand dynamics.

Liquidity
They provide liquidity, enabling investors to buy and sell assets easily and quickly without significant price changes.

Capital Formation
By facilitating the raising of capital, financial markets support business expansion and economic growth.

Risk Management

Derivatives and other financial instruments allow investors to hedge against risks such as price fluctuations in commodities or interest rate changes.

Efficient Allocation of Resources

Financial markets allocate capital to its most productive uses, promoting economic efficiency.

Participants in Financial Markets

Investors

Individuals or institutions that invest money in financial instruments to earn returns.

Issuers

Entities such as companies or governments that issue securities to raise capital.

Intermediaries

Financial institutions like banks, brokers, and mutual funds that facilitate transactions between buyers and sellers.

Regulators

Government agencies and regulatory bodies that oversee financial markets to ensure fairness, transparency, and stability. Examples include the Securities and Exchange Commission (SEC) in the United States and the Financial Conduct Authority (FCA) in the United Kingdom.

Financial markets are vital for economic development, providing mechanisms for raising capital, transferring risk, and ensuring liquidity. Understanding their structure, functions, and participants is essential for anyone involved in finance, investing, or business.

FINANCIAL MARKETS OVERVIEW

The financial markets consist of various types of markets where assets are bought and sold, including stocks, bonds, commodities, and currencies. Here's an overview of the key components:

Stock Markets

Overview: Platforms where shares of publicly traded companies are bought and sold. Major exchanges include the New York Stock Exchange (NYSE) and the Nasdaq.

Recent Trends: As of 2024, markets are influenced by factors like interest rate changes by central banks, geopolitical tensions, and corporate earnings reports. Key Indices: S&P 500, Dow Jones Industrial Average (DJIA), Nasdaq Composite.

Bond Markets

Overview: Markets for debt securities where investors can buy bonds issued by governments or corporations.

booksasasubject.store

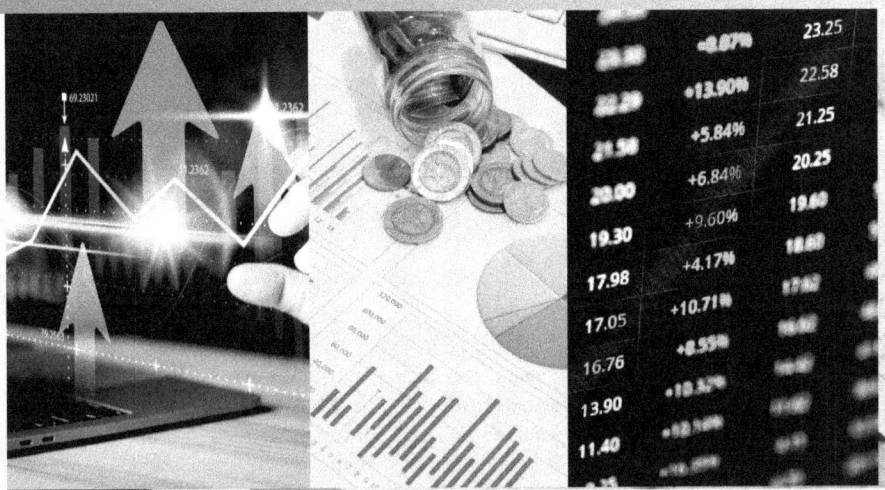

FINANCIAL MARKETS OVERVIEW

ent Trends: Interest rate fluctuations, particularly decisions by the Federal Reserve and other central banks, significantly impact bond prices. As of 2024, there has been a trend of rising interest rates.

Key Instruments: Treasury

Commodities Markets Overview: Markets where raw or primary products are exchanged. Commodities can be divided into two main categories: hard commodities (natural resources) and soft commodities (agricultural products). Recent Trends: Commodity prices are influenced by supply and demand dynamics, geopolitical events, and weather conditions. In 2024, energy prices (oil and gas) and agricultural products have seen significant volatility. Key Commodities: Oil, gold, silver, agricultural products (wheat, corn).

Foreign Exchange Markets (Forex)

Overview: The global marketplace for buying and selling currencies. It is the largest financial market in the world.

Recent Trends: Currency values are affected by interest rate differentials, economic data releases, and geopolitical events. As of 2024, the US dollar has experienced fluctuations due to changing economic policies and global trade dynamics.

Major Currencies: US Dollar (USD), Euro (EUR), Japanese Yen (JPY), British Pound (GBP).

Derivatives Markets

Overview: Financial instruments deriving their value from an underlying asset, such as options, futures, and swaps.

Recent Trends: Used for hedging and speculative purposes, derivatives markets are influenced by volatility in the underlying assets. In 2024, increased market volatility has led to higher trading volumes in derivatives.

Key Instruments: Futures contracts, options, swaps.

Cryptocurrency Markets

Overview: Digital or virtual currencies that use cryptography for security. Bitcoin and Ethereum are the most prominent examples.

Recent Trends: Cryptocurrency markets are highly volatile and influenced by regulatory developments, technological advancements, and market sentiment. In 2024, there has been a focus on regulatory scrutiny and the integration of blockchain technology in various industries.

Major Cryptocurrencies: Bitcoin (BTC), Ethereum (ETH), Binance Coin (BNB), Ripple (XRP).

Key Factors Influencing Financial Markets in 2024: Monetary Policy: Central bank policies, especially interest rate changes by the Federal Reserve, European Central Bank, etc. Geopolitical Events: Tensions and conflicts can lead to market volatility. Economic Indicators: Data such as GDP growth, unemployment rates, and inflation. Corporate Earnings: Quarterly earnings reports from major corporations. Technological Innovations: Advancements, particularly in fintech and blockchain.

Conclusion The financial markets are interconnected and influenced by a complex web of factors. Staying informed about global events, economic indicators, and market trends is crucial for investors and market participants.

HISTORY

The history of financial markets is a long and complex story that reflects the development of economies, societies, and technologies over millennia. Here's a high-level overview: Ancient and Mediaeval Periods Early Trading Systems: Barter System: The earliest form of trading involved bartering goods and services directly without a common medium of exchange. Commodity Money: Precious metals like gold and silver began to be used as money due to their inherent value and portability. Ancient Markets: Mesopotamia: Early evidence of commodity markets can be traced back to ancient Mesopotamia around 3000 BCE, where barley and silver were used as standardised forms of money. Greece and Rome: These civilizations developed more sophisticated financial systems, including the use of coins and the establishment of banks.

Mediaeval Period: Mediaeval Fairs: In Europe, mediaeval fairs became centres for trade, where merchants from different regions would gather. Early Banks: The Medici family in Italy established one of the first banking systems, facilitating trade and the flow of capital across Europe.

Early Modern Period Birth of Stock Exchanges: Amsterdam Stock Exchange: Established in 1602, it is often considered the world's first official stock exchange, where shares of the Dutch East India Company were traded. London Stock Exchange: Originated in 1698 in London, it became a major financial centre, formalising the trading of stocks and bonds. Development of Financial Instruments: Government Bonds: Governments began issuing bonds to finance wars and other expenditures. Joint-Stock Companies: These allowed for the pooling of capital for large ventures, reducing individual risk. 19th Century ndustrial Revolution: The explosion of industrial activity increased the need for capital, leading to the growth of stock markets. New York Stock Exchange: Established in 1817, it became a key player in global finance.

Panic and Crashes: Panic of 1837: A financial crisis in the U.S. caused by speculative lending practices, leading to a severe economic depression. Panic of 1873: Triggered by the collapse of the railroad industry and leading to a long economic depression.

20th Century The Great Depression: 1929 Stock Market Crash: This major collapse of stock prices marked the beginning of the Great Depression, leading to widespread economic hardship. Regulatory Reforms: In response, the U.S. government introduced the Securities Act of 1933 and the Securities Exchange Act of 1934 to regulate the markets. Post-War Expansion: Economic Boom: The post-World War II period saw significant economic growth and the expansion of financial markets. Bretton Woods System: Established in 1944, it created fixed exchange rates and the International Monetary Fund (IMF) to stabilise global economies. Technological Advances: Electronic Trading: The introduction of computers revolutionised trading, leading to the creation of electronic stock exchanges like NASDAQ in 1971.

INTRODUCTION

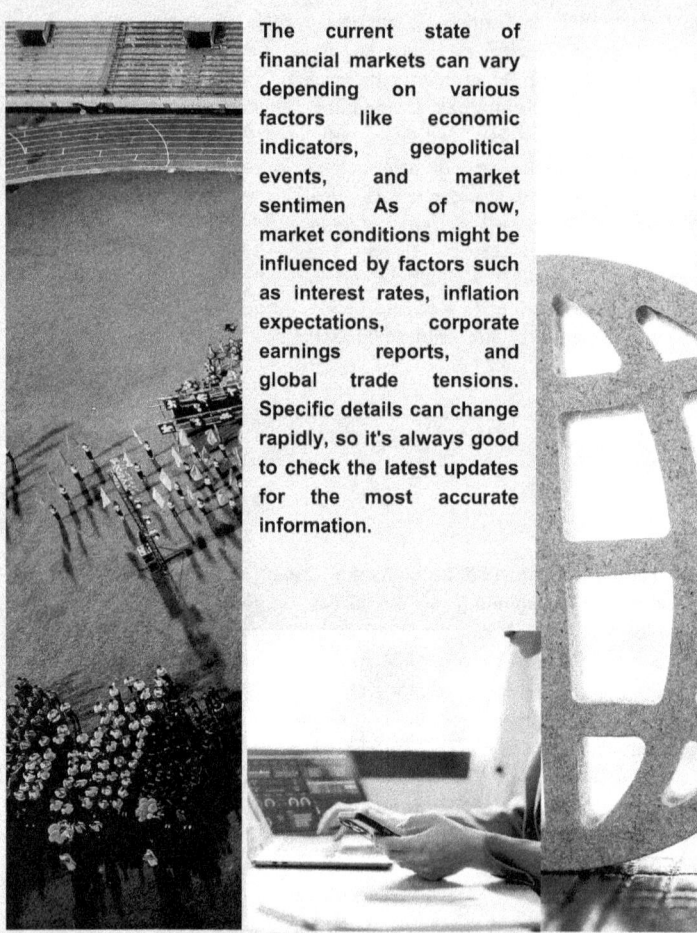

The current state of financial markets can vary depending on various factors like economic indicators, geopolitical events, and market sentimen As of now, market conditions might be influenced by factors such as interest rates, inflation expectations, corporate earnings reports, and global trade tensions. Specific details can change rapidly, so it's always good to check the latest updates for the most accurate information.

booksasasubject.store

FUTURE

The future of financial markets is always a topic of interest and speculation. Some key trends and factors likely to shape their trajectory include:
Technology and Innovation: Continued advancements in fintech, blockchain, AI, and big data analytics are expected to transform how financial services are delivered and consumed. Regulation: Regulatory changes globally can impact market stability, investor confidence, and the adoption of new technologies.
Global Economic Trends: Economic growth, inflation rates, and geopolitical developments influence market sentiment and investment decisions.
Sustainability and ESG: Increasing focus on environmental, social, and governance (ESG) factors is reshaping investment strategies and market dynamics.

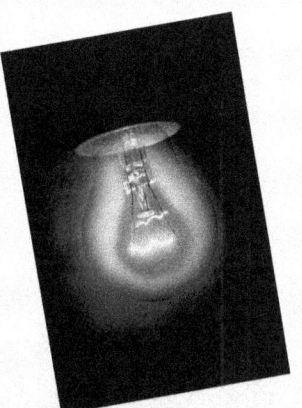

Cryptocurrencies and Digital Assets: The evolution and regulation of cryptocurrencies and digital assets are likely to impact traditional financial markets.

Demographics: Ageing populations, wealth transfer to younger generations, and shifting consumer behaviours are reshaping market demands.

booksasasubject.store

TENDER AGE (CHILDHOOD TO TEENAGE YEARS)

Financial Literacy Starting to learn about financial markets at a young age can significantly contribute to financial literacy and long-term financial well-being. Here are some reasons why early education in financial markets is beneficial: Foundation of Knowledge Basic Concepts Early exposure to financial markets helps young individuals grasp fundamental concepts such as stocks, bonds, interest rates, and diversification. Understanding Risks and Rewards Learning about the potential gains and risks associated with different investments helps in developing a balanced perspective on financial decision-making. Developing Good Habits Saving and Investing Early education encourages the habit of saving and investing, fostering a mindset that prioritises long-term financial goals over immediate gratification. Budgeting Understanding financial markets can enhance budgeting skills, as individuals learn to allocate resources efficiently and plan for future expenses.

booksasasubject.store

Critical Thinking and Decision-Making Informed Choices Knowledge of financial markets enables young people to make informed decisions about their personal finances, including choosing investments and managing debt. Analytical Skills Analysing market trends and financial statements develops critical thinking skills that are applicable in various aspects of life. Preparation for Adulthood Financial Independence Early financial education prepares individuals for financial independence by equipping them with the skills to manage their own finances responsibly. Avoiding Debt Understanding the implications of borrowing and the importance of credit scores helps in avoiding excessive debt and managing credit wisely. Economic Awareness Global Economy Learning about financial markets provides insight into how the global economy operates, fostering a broader understanding of economic principles and current events. Financial News Being able to interpret financial news and its impact on personal finances is a valuable skill that aids in making timely and informed decisions. Building Confidence Empowerment Financial literacy empowers young individuals by giving them the knowledge and confidence to take control of their financial future. Reducing Anxiety A solid understanding of financial markets can reduce anxiety about money matters, as individuals feel more capable of handling financial Long-Term Benefits Compounding Returns Early investment in financial literacy allows individuals to take advantage of the power of compounding returns over a longer period, potentially leading to greater wealth accumulation. Career Opportunities A strong foundation in financial markets can open up various career opportunities in finance, investment, banking, and related fields. Responsibility and Discipline Accountability Learning about financial markets instils a sense of responsibility and discipline in managing money, leading to better financial habits and decision-making. Starting financial education at a young age sets the stage for lifelong financial literacy, enabling individuals to navigate the complexities of the financial world with confidence and competence.

Critical Thinking and Problem-Solving Starting to learn about financial markets at a young age can significantly enhance critical thinking and problem-solving skills for several reasons: Complex Concepts and Analysis Understanding financial markets involves grasping complex concepts such as supply and demand, market trends, and economic indicators. This requires the ability to analyse and interpret data, fostering critical thinking. Decision Making Financial markets are unpredictable and involve making decisions based on incomplete information. Young learners must evaluate risks and potential outcomes, which enhances their problem-solving abilities. Real-World Applications Financial education connects theoretical knowledge with real-world scenarios. This practical application encourages learners to think critically about how financial principles apply to everyday life. Pattern Recognition Recognizing trends and patterns in financial data helps develop analytical skills. Identifying these patterns requires observation, hypothesis testing, and logical reasoning, all of which are key components of critical thinking. Strategic Thinking Investing and trading require strategic planning and forward-thinking. Young learners develop the ability to anticipate market movements and plan their actions accordingly, which strengthens problem-solving skills. Adaptability Financial markets are dynamic and constantly changing. Learning to adapt to new information and adjust strategies in response to market fluctuations builds resilience and flexible thinking. Numeracy Skills Financial markets involve a lot of quantitative analysis. Developing strong numeracy skills early on can improve overall cognitive abilities and support other areas of critical thinking and problem-solving. Informed Decision-Making Making informed decisions based on market analysis teaches young learners to weigh evidence, consider multiple perspectives, and make reasoned judgments. Ethical Considerations Understanding financial markets also involves grappling with ethical issues related to investments, corporate behaviour, and economic impacts. This encourages young learners to think critically about ethical dilemmas and develop a strong moral compass. Global Awareness Financial markets are interconnected globally. Learning about them fosters an understanding of global economics, politics, and cultural impacts, broadening perspectives and enhancing critical thinking about world issues. Starting financial education at a young age not only builds a foundation for financial literacy but also equips learners with essential skills that are applicable across various aspects of life and career.

booksasasubject.store

Responsibility and Discipline Starting to learn about financial markets at a tender age fosters responsibility and discipline for several reasons. Early Habit Formation Learning about financial markets early helps in establishing good financial habits. These habits, such as budgeting, saving, and investing, require regular practice and commitment, instilling discipline over time. Long-term Perspective Financial markets inherently require a long-term perspective. Young learners develop patience and the understanding that significant financial growth often takes time, which fosters discipline in maintaining long-term financial strategies. Risk Management Understanding financial markets involves learning about risks and how to manage them. This teaches responsibility in decision-making, as young individuals learn to evaluate potential risks and rewards before taking action. Financial Literacy Gaining knowledge about financial markets improves overall financial literacy. This empowers young individuals to make informed decisions about their finances, leading to responsible money management. Goal Setting and Planning investing in financial markets involves setting financial goals and creating plans to achieve them. Young learners who engage in this practice develop the discipline to plan for the future and the responsibility to follow through with their plans. Accountability Tracking investments and financial performance requires regular review and adjustment. This process teaches young individuals to be accountable for their financial decisions and actions. Self-Control Successful investing often means resisting impulsive decisions based on market fluctuations. Learning this self-control early can help in other areas of life where patience and thoughtful decision-making are crucial. Understanding Consequences Young learners who invest can experience the direct consequences of their financial decisions, both positive and negative. This hands-on experience reinforces the importance of responsibility and discipline in financial management. Starting financial education early equips individuals with the skills and mindset needed to navigate the complexities of financial markets responsibly and with discipline, laying a strong foundation for their financial future.

Future Preparedness
Starting to learn about financial markets at a tender age can significantly contribute to future preparedness for several reasons.

Compound Knowledge
Similar to compound interest, knowledge builds over time. Starting young allows individuals to accumulate a wealth of knowledge and experience that can be extremely valuable as they grow older.

The Power of Compounding
Starting to learn about financial markets at a tender age can significantly harness the power of compounding. Here's an elaborate explanation:

Understanding the Power of Compounding
Compounding is the process where the value of an investment increases because the earnings on an investment, both capital gains and interest, earn interest as time passes. In simpler terms, it's earning interest on interest, leading to exponential growth of your investment over time.

Early Start Maximises Time
Longer Time Horizon: Starting early gives your investments more time to grow. Compounding works best over long periods. The earlier you start, the more you benefit from the exponential growth.

Example: If you invest $1,000 at the age of 20 at an annual return rate of 7%, it will grow to about $38,000 by the age of 65. If you start at 30, it will grow to only around $19,000 by the age of 65. The extra ten years make a significant difference due to compounding.

Incremental Learning and Better Decision-Making
Knowledge Accumulation: Starting young allows for incremental learning and better understanding of financial markets. This knowledge helps in making informed investment decisions, which is crucial for maximising returns.

Risk Management: Young investors can afford to take more risks since they have more time to recover from potential losses. As they age, they can shift to more stable investments.

Consistency and Habit Formation

Regular Investments: Learning early instils the habit of regular investing. Consistently investing small amounts over time can lead to significant growth due to compounding.

Financial Discipline: Early education in financial markets promotes financial discipline and better money management skills, leading to a more secure financial future.

Leveraging Market Opportunities

Market Fluctuations: Young investors can take advantage of market fluctuations and downturns. They have the flexibility to buy low and hold until the market recovers, benefiting from the higher returns during market upswings.

Diversification: They have more time to diversify their portfolios and experiment with different asset classes, further enhancing the potential for compounded growth.

Inflation Beating Real Value Growth: Over time, inflation erodes the purchasing power of money. Investments that compound at a rate higher than inflation ensure that the real value of your money grows, safeguarding against inflation. Starting to learn and invest in financial markets at a young age leverages the power of compounding, which is fundamental to building substantial wealth over time. The earlier one starts, the more they benefit from the exponential growth of their investments, making financial security and wealth accumulation more achievable. Financial Literacy Early exposure to financial concepts fosters a strong foundation in financial literacy. This understanding can lead to better financial decisions, such as saving, investing, and budgeting, throughout life. Risk Management Understanding financial markets at a young age helps individuals learn about risk and how to manage it. This can lead to more informed and less emotional decision-making during financial market fluctuations. Economic Awareness Learning about financial markets includes understanding broader economic principles and global economic events. This awareness can enhance an individual's ability to navigate the complexities of the global economy. Investment Skills Starting early allows individuals to practise and refine their investment strategies over time. This long-term experience can improve their ability to make sound investment choices and increase their wealth. Career Opportunities Knowledge of financial markets can open doors to various career opportunities in finance, economics, and related fields. It can also provide a competitive edge in many other professions. Financial Independence Early financial education can lead to habits that promote financial independence, such as saving regularly, avoiding debt, and understanding the importance of building an emergency fund. Confidence and Discipline Learning and experiencing financial markets helps build confidence in managing personal finances. It also instils discipline in financial habits, which can be beneficial throughout life. Entrepreneurial Skills Knowledge of financial markets can enhance entrepreneurial skills by providing insights into funding, capital markets, and financial planning, which are crucial for running a successful business. Adaptability Early exposure to financial markets can teach individuals how to adapt to changes in the economic environment, which is a valuable skill in an ever-evolving financial landscape.

booksasasubject.store

Learning Through Play: Financial Games and Simulations Starting to learn about financial markets at a young age through financial games and simulations can be highly beneficial for several reasons. Here's an elaboration on why this approach can be effective: Early Familiarity with Financial Concepts Foundation Building: Introducing financial markets early helps children build a strong foundation in basic financial concepts such as saving, investing, and budgeting. Understanding these concepts early can make them more comfortable and confident when dealing with financial matters as they grow older. Cognitive Development: Young brains are highly adaptable and capable of learning complex concepts quickly. Early exposure to financial concepts can take advantage of this cognitive flexibility. Engaging Learning Methods interactive Learning: Financial games and simulations are interactive, making learning about financial markets engaging and enjoyable. This can help maintain a child's interest and curiosity. Practical Application: These tools often simulate real-world scenarios, allowing children to apply theoretical knowledge in a practical setting. This can enhance their understanding and retention of financial concepts. Development of Critical Thinking and Decision-Making Skills Problem Solving: Financial games require players to make decisions based on available information, promoting critical thinking and problem-solving skills. Risk Management: Children learn to assess risks and rewards, a crucial skill in financial markets. They can experiment with different strategies in a safe environment without real-world consequences. Fostering Financial Responsibility Understanding Consequences: Simulations can show the consequences of financial decisions, helping children understand the importance of financial responsibility and planning. Goal Setting: Games often involve setting and achieving financial goals, teaching children the value of goal setting and persistence. Encouraging a Growth Mindset Learning from Mistakes: Financial games provide a safe space for children to make mistakes and learn from them. This encourages a growth mindset, where mistakes are seen as opportunities for learning rather than failures. Adaptability: By navigating various financial scenarios, children learn to adapt to changing circumstances, a valuable skill in the ever-evolving financial markets. Integration of Technology and Finance Digital Literacy: Using digital tools for financial simulations helps children become comfortable with technology, which is increasingly important in modern financial markets. Accessibility: Many financial games and simulations are available online, making them easily accessible and convenient for continuous learning

Building Confidence and Independence Empowerment: Knowledge about financial markets empowers children to make informed decisions about their money. This can lead to greater financial independence as they grow older. Confidence Boost: Successfully navigating financial games can boost a child's confidence in their ability to manage financial matters. Social and Collaborative Learning Peer Interaction: Many financial games can be played in groups, encouraging collaboration and communication. Children can learn from each other and develop teamwork skills. Competitive Spirit: Friendly competition in games can motivate children to improve their financial knowledge and skills. By integrating financial markets education with play, children can develop a strong, practical understanding of finance in an engaging and supportive environment. This early start can set the stage for lifelong financial literacy and competence. Early Savings: Piggy Banks to Junior Accounts Starting to learn about financial markets at a tender age can have a profound impact on fostering early savings habits, transitioning from simple piggy banks to more sophisticated junior accounts. Here's an elaboration on why this is beneficial: Building Financial Literacy Understanding Money Management Early exposure to financial concepts helps children understand the value of money, the importance of saving, and the basics of budgeting. Concepts of Interest and Investment Introducing concepts like interest, compounding, and investment early on can demystify the financial markets and encourage informed decisions in the future. Instilling Good Habits Savings Discipline Starting with something as simple as a piggy bank can instil the habit of setting aside money regularly. Progression to Junior Accounts As children grow, transitioning from piggy banks to junior savings accounts teaches them about banking, interest earnings, and financial responsibility. Encouraging Goal Setting .Short-term and Long-term Goals Learning about financial markets encourages setting financial goals, whether it's saving for a toy or understanding long-term investments for education. Financial Planning This goal-setting can translate into better financial planning skills as they mature, ensuring they are prepared for future financial needs.

YOUTH (20S TO EARLY 30S)

Time Advantag Starting to learn about financial markets in your youth (20s to early 30s) provides a significant time advantage due to several key reasons : Compound Interest Early Start Beginning to invest early allows your money to benefit from compound interest over a longer period. Compound interest is the process where the interest earned on an investment itself earns interest. The earlier you start, the more time your investments have to grow exponentially. Example If you invest $1,000 at an annual return rate of 7% at age 25, it will grow to about $7,612 by age 65. If you start investing the same amount at age 35, it will grow to about $3,870 by age 65. Risk Tolerance Higher Risk Capacity Younger individuals can typically afford to take more risks with their investments because they have a longer time horizon to recover from potential losses. This allows for investments in higher-risk, higher-reward assets. Learning from Mistakes Early investing allows you to learn from mistakes and adjust strategies without the immediate pressure of needing funds for retirement or other major expenses. Long-term Planning Financial Goals Starting early provides more time to plan and achieve long-term financial goals, such as buying a house, funding education, or planning for retirement. With a longer time frame, you can set more realistic and achievable goals.

Cost Averaging By investing regularly over a long period, you can take advantage of dollar-cost averaging, which can reduce the impact of market volatility on your portfolio. Economic Cycles Experiencing Market Cycles Over a longer period, you will experience various market cycles, including booms and busts. This experience can provide valuable insights and help you become a more informed and resilient investor. Patience and Discipline Investing over decades instils patience and discipline, which are crucial traits for successful investing. Education and Skill Development Learning Curve The earlier you start, the more time you have to educate yourself about financial markets, investment strategies, and economic principles. This knowledge can significantly enhance your ability to make informed decisions. Building Expertise Continuous learning and experience over many years can turn you into an expert, potentially leading to better investment decisions and financial outcomes. Starting early increases the chances of achieving financial independence at a younger age, giving you more freedom to pursue personal goals and interests without financial constraints. Retirement Savings Consistent investing from a young age can lead to a substantial retirement nest egg, providing financial security in your later years. Tax Advantages Tax-Advantaged Accounts Contributing to tax-advantaged accounts like IRAs and 401(k)s from a young age maximises the benefits of tax deferral and employer matching contributions, further boosting your investment growth. starting to learn about and invest in financial markets early in life leverages the power of compound interest, allows for greater risk tolerance, and provides ample time to develop financial literacy and experience. This time advantage significantly enhances your potential for long-term financial success and stability. Risk Tolerance Starting to learn about financial markets in your youth (20s to early 30s) can significantly enhance risk tolerance for several reasons. Time Horizon Long-Term Perspective Young investors have a longer time horizon before retirement, allowing them to take on more risk because they have more time to recover from potential losses.

booksasasubject.store

Compounding Starting early takes advantage of compound interest, where returns on investments generate their own returns over time, amplifying growth. Learning and Adaptation Experience Early exposure to financial markets allows individuals to gain valuable experience, understand market fluctuations, and learn from both successes and mistakes. Skill Development Over time, young investors can develop sophisticated skills in analysing markets, understanding economic indicators, and making informed decisions. Psychological Benefits Risk Tolerance Development Experiencing market volatility early helps build a psychological tolerance to risk, reducing fear and improving confidence in handling investments during downturns. Emotional Resilience Learning to manage emotions and maintain a long-term perspective during market swings can lead to better investment decisions. Financial Security Wealth Accumulation Starting early increases the potential for wealth accumulation, providing a cushion that can enhance risk tolerance. Diverse Portfolio With time, young investors can build a diversified portfolio, spreading risk across different asset classes and reducing overall risk exposure. Opportunity to Take Risks Aggressive Growth Younger investors can afford to allocate a larger portion of their portfolio to high-risk, high-reward investments because they have time to recover from potential losses. Learning Curve The ability to take risks early on means they can learn from these experiences and adjust strategies accordingly, leading to smarter risk management in the future. Flexibility and Adaptability Career and Income Growth Younger individuals are typically in the early stages of their careers, with potential for significant income growth, which can support higher risk investments. Life Changes Fewer financial responsibilities (e.g., no mortgage or children) allow for more flexibility in investment choices and risk-taking.

Technological and Educational Resources Access to Information Young investors today have unprecedented access to educational resources, online courses, and real-time market information, facilitating informed decision-making. Investment Tools Modern technology provides sophisticated tools and platforms that help young investors manage and mitigate risks effectively. Starting to learn about financial markets in your youth not only enhances risk tolerance but also provides a solid foundation for long-term financial stability and growth. The combination of a long time horizon, learning opportunities, psychological resilience, and flexibility allows young investors to take calculated risks and potentially achieve greater financial success. Risk and Reward: Learning from Mistakes Starting to learn about financial markets in your youth, particularly in your 20s to early 30s, can bring about both risks and rewards. Here's an elaboration on how this period allows for learning from mistakes and the associated benefits: Time to Recover from Mistakes Risk When you are young, you might make investment mistakes due to a lack of experience and knowledge. These mistakes can lead to financial losses. Reward Because you have a longer investment horizon, you have more time to recover from these mistakes. The financial markets tend to have cyclical patterns, and over time, well-placed investments can rebound and grow. Early mistakes provide valuable lessons without derailing long-term financial goals. Higher Risk Tolerance Risk Younger investors may be more prone to taking higher risks due to overconfidence or a lack of understanding of market volatility. This can lead to significant short-term losses. Reward Higher risk tolerance can also lead to higher potential returns. Younger investors can afford to take on more aggressive investment strategies that might not be suitable for older individuals closer to retirement. Over time, the ability to take on more risk can lead to substantial wealth accumulation. Compound Interest and Long-Term Growth Risk Misunderstanding the power of compound interest can lead to underutilization of this powerful financial tool. Poor investment choices early on can hinder the benefits of compounding.

Reward Starting early allows investments to grow exponentially through compound interest. Even if early investments are modest, the compounding effect over several decades can lead to significant wealth. Early lessons learned from mistakes can be applied to improve future investment decisions, enhancing long-term growth. Developing Financial Discipline Risk Inexperience can lead to impulsive financial decisions, such as frequent trading or chasing market trends, which can erode returns and increase transaction costs. Reward Learning from these mistakes can help develop financial discipline and a more strategic, long-term approach to investing. Young investors can develop habits such as regular saving, investing consistently, and avoiding emotional reactions to market fluctuations. Building a Knowledge Base Risk Initial lack of knowledge about financial markets can lead to misguided investments, following poor advice, or falling prey to market speculation and scams. Reward Early experiences, even if they involve mistakes, contribute to building a solid knowledge base about financial markets. Over time, young investors can become more adept at analysing market trends, understanding financial statements, and making informed investment decisions. This knowledge can lead to more strategic and less risky investments in the future. Flexibility and Adaptability Risk Early in their investing journey, young individuals might not have a clear understanding of their risk tolerance and financial goals, leading to a mismatch in investment choices. Reward Youth provides the flexibility to adapt and change investment strategies as one learns and as personal circumstances evolve. Early mistakes provide critical feedback, helping young investors better understand their own risk tolerance and refine their financial goals over time. Starting to learn about financial markets in your youth offers a unique opportunity to experience both risks and rewards. The key advantage is the ability to make and learn from mistakes without the immediate pressure of retirement looming. This period allows for the development of critical financial skills, knowledge, and discipline, all of which contribute to a more secure and prosperous financial future.

Skill Development Starting to learn about financial markets in your youth, particularly in your 20s to early 30s, can significantly enhance skill development for several reasons: Foundation of Knowledge Basic Financial Literacy Understanding concepts like savings, investments, interest rates, and financial planning. Complex Financial Instruments Learning about stocks, bonds, mutual funds, ETFs, and derivatives provides a deeper understanding of financial markets. Analytical Skills Data Interpretation Analysing financial statements, market trends, and economic indicators. Critical Thinking Evaluating investment opportunities and making informed decisions based on market conditions and company performance. Technical Skills Technology Proficiency Using financial tools and platforms such as trading software, financial modelling tools, and online research databases. Quantitative Skills: Developing abilities in mathematics and statistics to understand and predict market movements. Decision-Making Skills Risk Management Learning to assess and mitigate financial risks, understanding the trade-offs between risk and return. Strategic Planning Setting financial goals, creating investment strategies, and adapting to market changes. Economic Understanding Global Perspective Understanding how global events impact financial markets, including political changes, economic policies, and international trade. Macroeconomic Indicators Recognizing the influence of inflation, interest rates, and GDP growth on financial markets. Personal Development Discipline and Patience Investing requires a long-term perspective, teaching patience and the importance of disciplined saving and investing habits. Financial Independence Early knowledge and experience can lead to better financial independence and security.

Professional Opportunities Career Advancement Skills in financial markets can lead to careers in finance, banking, investment, and other related fields. Networking Engaging with financial professionals and joining financial communities can open doors to mentorship and career opportunities. Adaptability and Continuous Learning Staying Informed The financial markets are dynamic, requiring continuous learning and adaptation to new information and trends. Problem-Solving Developing the ability to solve complex financial problems and adapt strategies as needed. Entrepreneurial Skills Business Acumen Understanding how financial markets impact business operations, funding, and growth strategies. Innovation and Strategy Identifying new market opportunities and creating innovative financial products or services. Confidence and Empowerment Informed Decisions Confidence in making informed financial decisions, from personal investments to professional ventures. Empowerment Empowerment to take control of one's financial future and make proactive financial choices. Starting to learn about financial markets early in life equips individuals with a robust skill set that not only enhances their financial acumen but also provides a competitive edge in their personal and professional lives.

ADULTHOOD (30S TO EARLY 50S

Wealth Accumulation Starting to learn about financial markets during youth (30s to early 50s) can significantly contribute to wealth accumulation for several reasons. Here's a detailed explanation: Time Advantage Compounding Starting early allows more time for investments to grow and benefit from compound interest. The longer the investment period, the more substantial the effects of compounding, where returns generate their own returns. Risk Tolerance Younger individuals typically have a higher risk tolerance, enabling them to invest in higher-risk, higher-reward assets. Over time, the likelihood of achieving higher returns increases. Knowledge and Experience Learning Curve The financial markets are complex. Starting early provides ample time to understand different investment vehicles, market cycles, and economic indicators. Experience gained over the years can lead to more informed and strategic investment decisions. Mistake Recovery Making mistakes is part of the learning process. Younger investors have more time to recover from poor decisions and market downturns, allowing them to adjust strategies and improve.

booksasasubject.store

Income Growth and Investment Capacity Earnings Potential People in their 30s to early 50s are typically in their prime earning years. Higher income allows for greater investment capacity and the ability to take advantage of market opportunities. Lifestyle Adjustments At this stage, individuals often have more flexibility to make lifestyle adjustments that can free up additional funds for investing, such as reducing discretionary spending. Diversification and Asset Allocation Time to Diversify Starting early allows investors to gradually diversify their portfolios. They can allocate assets across different classes such as stocks, bonds, real estate, and alternative investments, reducing risk. Adjustment of Allocation As market conditions and personal circumstances change, early starters have the flexibility to adjust their asset allocation to optimise returns and manage risk. Long-Term Goals and Planning Retirement Planning Learning about financial markets early provides the knowledge and tools needed to plan effectively for retirement. This includes understanding different retirement accounts, tax implications, and withdrawal strategies. Goal Setting Early investors can set long-term financial goals, such as buying a home, funding education, or starting a business. Understanding financial markets helps in creating and following a strategic plan to achieve these goals. Psychological Benefits Confidence Gaining knowledge and experience in financial markets builds confidence in managing personal finances. This confidence can lead to more proactive and disciplined financial habits. Reduced Stress Financial literacy can reduce anxiety about money by providing a clearer understanding of how to grow and protect wealth. Informed Voting and Advocacy Financial literacy empowers individuals to make informed decisions about economic policies and regulations. This can influence voting behaviour and advocacy for policies that promote financial stability and growth.

Community Impact Financially literate individuals can contribute to the economic well-being of their communities by making informed investments and supporting local businesses. In summary, starting to learn about financial markets in one's 30s to early 50s leverages the advantages of time, income, and risk tolerance. It provides the foundation for informed decision-making, effective planning, and long-term wealth accumulation. Retirement Planning Learning about financial markets starting in your youth (30s to early 50s) can significantly enhance retirement planning. Here are several reasons why: Time to Accumulate Wealth Compound Interest The earlier you start investing, the more you benefit from compound interest. Over time, the interest earned on your investments starts to generate its own interest, leading to exponential growth. Long-Term Investment Starting early allows you to invest in long-term assets, such as stocks, which have historically provided higher returns over extended periods. Risk Management Market Fluctuations Younger investors have more time to ride out market volatility. This longer time horizon enables them to recover from market downturns and take advantage of growth periods. Diversification With more time, you can diversify your investments across various asset classes, reducing risk and increasing the potential for stable returns. Financial Literacy Understanding Markets Learning about financial markets helps you understand how different assets (stocks, bonds, real estate, etc.) perform and how they can be used to achieve your financial goals. nformed Decisions Greater knowledge leads to more informed investment decisions, reducing the likelihood of panic selling during downturns or making poor investment choices. Building a Solid Foundatio Savings Discipline Starting early helps build a habit of saving and investing regularly, which is crucial for accumulating wealth over time. Emergency Funds Knowledge of financial markets also encourages the establishment of emergency funds, providing a safety net that prevents the need to dip into retirement savings.34

Maximising Retirement Accounts Tax Advantages Many retirement accounts, such as 401(k)s and IRAs, offer tax benefits. Understanding how these work allows you to maximise contributions and take full advantage of employer matches and tax-deferred growth Catch-Up Contributions As you approach your 50s, you can make catch-up contributions to retirement accounts, significantly boosting your retirement savings. Adjusting Goals and Strategies Reevaluating Goals Starting early gives you the flexibility to periodically reassess and adjust your retirement goals and investment strategies based on changing circumstances. Adapting to Life Changes Whether it's a career change, family expansion, or economic shifts, having a strong understanding of financial markets enables you to adapt your retirement plan accordingly. Peace of Mind Financial Security Knowing that you have a well-thought-out plan for retirement provides peace of mind. You can enjoy your working years and retirement without the constant stress of financial uncertainty. Legacy Planning Early and informed investment also allows for better planning in terms of leaving a legacy for your loved ones or charitable causes. Starting to learn about financial markets in your 30s to early 50s equips you with the knowledge and tools necessary for effective retirement planning. This proactive approach not only increases your potential for wealth accumulation but also provides a foundation for making informed decisions, managing risk, and securing a comfortable retirement. Starting to Invest: 401(k)s, IRAs, and Other Retirement Plans Learning about financial markets and starting to invest in retirement plans like 401(k)s, IRAs, and other vehicles early in life (from the 30s to early 50s) offers several advantages: Time Horizon for Compounding Starting early allows your investments more time to grow through compounding. Compounding means that your investment returns earn returns themselves, amplifying your wealth over time. The longer your money is invested, the more significant this effect becomes. Risk Management Investing early gives you more time to recover from any potential losses. Financial markets can be volatile in the short term, but historically they tend to trend upwards over the long term. Starting young allows you to weather these fluctuations and benefit from overall market growth.

Tax Advantages Retirement plans like 401(k)s and IRAs offer tax advantages such as tax-deferred or tax-free growth. Contributions to these accounts can also lower your taxable income in the year you make them, potentially reducing your current tax burden. Building Discipline Learning about financial markets and investing early instils financial discipline and good habits. It encourages regular saving and investing, which are crucial for long-term financial security. Retirement Readiness By starting to invest early, you're actively preparing for retirement. Building a substantial nest egg takes time, and starting early gives you a better chance of achieving your retirement goals and maintaining your desired lifestyle post-retirement. Diversification and Asset Allocation Learning about financial markets helps you understand the importance of diversification and asset allocation. These strategies can help manage risk while maximising potential returns based on your risk tolerance and financial goals. Overall, starting to learn about financial markets and investing early empowers you to make informed decisions, take advantage of compounding growth, manage risks effectively, and build a solid foundation for your future financial well-being. Financial Goals Starting to learn about financial markets in your 30s to early 50s can be a crucial step toward achieving financial goals for several reasons: Time Horizon for Compounding Compounding Effect The earlier you start investing, the more time your investments have to grow through the power of compounding. Compounding is the process where the returns on your investments generate their own returns over time. Long-Term Growth A longer investment horizon allows you to ride out market volatility and benefit from the long-term upward trend of financial markets. Accumulation Phase Peak Earning Years Individuals in their 30s to early 50s are often in their peak earning years. This provides an opportunity to allocate a higher portion of income toward investments. Higher Savings Potential With potentially higher incomes and fewer financial responsibilities than earlier in life, there is greater capacity to save and invest. Risk Tolerance and Management Risk Capacity Younger individuals generally have a higher risk tolerance because they have more time to recover from potential losses. This allows for a more aggressive investment strategy that can yield higher returns.

Learning and Adaptation Starting earlier gives you more time to learn about financial markets, understand different investment options, and develop strategies to manage risk effectively. Financial Literacy Building Knowledge Early education in financial markets helps build a strong foundation of financial literacy. Understanding concepts like asset allocation, diversification, and market cycles can lead to more informed and confident investment decisions. Avoiding Mistakes With more knowledge, you're better equipped to avoid common investment pitfalls, such as panic selling during market downturns or chasing high-risk, high-reward investments without proper due diligence. Goal Setting and Planning Clear Financial Goals Starting early allows you to define clear financial goals, such as buying a home, funding children's education, or planning for retirement. Strategic Planning With more time, you can develop and adjust a strategic investment plan to achieve these goals. This includes setting short-term and long-term objectives and regularly reviewing and rebalancing your portfolio. Tax Advantages Tax-Advantaged Accounts nvesting in tax-advantaged accounts like 401(k)s or IRAs early can provide significant tax benefits, such as tax-deferred growth or tax-free withdrawals in retirement. Tax Planning Understanding financial markets and investment strategies can help in efficient tax planning, minimising tax liabilities, and maximising after-tax returns. Wealth Accumulation and Security Building Wealth Consistent investing over a longer period is a proven method for building significant wealth. This accumulated wealth can provide financial security and the ability to meet various financial goals. Emergency Fund Early investments can also contribute to building an emergency fund, providing a financial cushion in case of unexpected expenses or job loss. Retirement Planning Securing Retirement Starting to invest early helps ensure that you have sufficient funds to support your desired lifestyle in retirement. Avoiding Shortfalls It reduces the risk of retirement shortfalls, ensuring you do not have to rely solely on social security or other uncertain income sources.34

Legacy Planning Wealth Transfer Accumulating wealth through informed investing allows you to plan for wealth transfer to future generations, ensuring financial stability for your family. Estate Planning Understanding financial markets and investments aids in effective estate planning, minimising estate taxes and maximising the inheritance for your beneficiaries. Learning about financial markets in your 30s to early 50s equips you with the knowledge, skills, and time necessary to make informed investment decisions. This proactive approach can significantly enhance your ability to achieve financial goals, secure your future, and build a legacy for the next generation. Inflation Protection Learning about financial markets in your youth (30s to early 50s) can provide significant inflation protection for several reasons: Understanding Inflation and Its Impact Awareness By learning about financial markets, you become aware of how inflation erodes purchasing power over time. This understanding is crucial for making informed investment decisions that aim to outpace inflation. Knowledge Knowledge of inflation's impact helps you make better decisions about saving and investing. For example, keeping money in low-interest savings accounts may not keep pace with inflation, leading to a loss of real value. Investment in Inflation-Protected Securities TIPS Treasury Inflation-Protected Securities (TIPS) are a type of government bond specifically designed to protect against inflation. Understanding financial markets can help you identify and invest in these securities. Inflation-Linked Bonds Some corporate and municipal bonds are also indexed to inflation, providing another option for inflation protection. Diversification of Investments Asset Allocation Learning about financial markets helps you diversify your portfolio across different asset classes (stocks, bonds, real estate, commodities). Diversification can mitigate the risk of inflation eroding the value of your investments. Real Assets Investing in real assets such as real estate and commodities (e.g., gold) can provide a hedge against inflation, as these tend to appreciate when inflation rises.

Equities and Inflation Stocks Historically, equities have provided returns that outpace inflation over the long term. Understanding which sectors and companies are likely to perform well in an inflationary environment can enhance your investment strategy. Dividend Stocks Investing in companies with a history of increasing dividends can provide a steady income stream that keeps up with or exceeds inflation. Active Management and Rebalancing Portfolio Management Learning about financial markets includes understanding how to actively manage and rebalance your portfolio. This can involve shifting investments to sectors that historically perform well during inflationary periods (e.g., commodities, energy). Market Trends Being informed about market trends and economic indicators helps you anticipate inflationary periods and adjust your investments accordingly. Investment Vehicles Mutual Funds and ETFs There are mutual funds and exchange-traded funds (ETFs) that focus on inflation-protected assets. Learning about these vehicles allows you to include them in your portfolio. Alternative Investments Understanding financial markets opens up opportunities to invest in alternative assets like private equity, hedge funds, and infrastructure, which can offer inflation protection. Long-Term Financial Planning Retirement Planning Starting early with financial market education allows for better retirement planning. By building a portfolio that includes inflation-protected investments, you can ensure your retirement savings maintain their purchasing power. Compounding Returns The earlier you start investing, the more you can benefit from compounding returns, which can help outpace inflation over time. Risk Management Hedging Strategies Knowledge of financial markets includes understanding and implementing hedging strategies to protect against inflation. This can include using options, futures, and other derivatives.

Economic Cycles Understanding the economic cycles and their impact on inflation can help you make proactive investment decisions to mitigate inflation risk. By starting early, individuals have more time to build a diversified portfolio, benefit from compounding returns, and adjust their investment strategies as needed to protect against the eroding effects of inflation. This proactive approach can lead to greater financial security and stability in the face of rising prices. Managing Student Loans and Other Debts Starting to learn about financial markets in one's youth (30s to early 50s) can significantly improve the management of student loans and other debts for several reasons: Enhanced Financial Literacy Understanding financial markets increases overall financial literacy. This knowledge helps individuals make informed decisions about managing debts, including student loans. They can better understand interest rates, loan terms, and repayment strategies, leading to more effective debt management. Investment Knowledge Learning about financial markets includes gaining insights into various investment opportunities. By investing wisely, individuals can potentially grow their wealth, creating additional resources to pay off student loans and other debts more quickly. Investments such as stocks, bonds, mutual funds, or real estate can provide returns that outpace loan interest rates. Budgeting and Financial Planning Knowledge of financial markets often involves learning about budgeting and financial planning. Effective budgeting helps individuals allocate funds efficiently, ensuring that they can make regular debt payments while still saving and investing for the future. Financial planning tools and strategies can also help prioritise debt repayment, reducing overall financial stress. Understanding Credit and Interest Rates A deeper understanding of financial markets helps individuals grasp how credit works and how interest rates are determined. This can lead to better credit management, allowing for refinancing options or consolidations at lower interest rates, ultimately reducing the cost of borrowing. Risk Management Knowledge of financial markets includes understanding risk and how to manage it. This can translate into better debt management by avoiding high-risk financial behaviours that could lead to increased debt or financial instability. It also encourages the use of insurance and other protective measures to safeguard against unforeseen financial setbacks.

Long-Term Financial Goals Learning about financial markets encourages setting long-term financial goals. By focusing on long-term wealth accumulation and financial stability, individuals can develop a strategic approach to debt repayment that aligns with their overall financial objectives. This helps in creating a balance between paying off debts and building a financial cushion for the future. Access to Financial Tools and Resources Individuals who are knowledgeable about financial markets are more likely to take advantage of financial tools and resources such as debt repayment calculators, financial advisors, and online financial management platforms. These tools can provide personalised strategies for managing student loans and other debts effectively. Behavioural Changes Understanding the importance of financial markets and their impact on personal finances can lead to positive behavioural changes. Individuals may become more disciplined in their spending, saving, and investing habits, all of which contribute to more effective debt management. Networking and Mentorship Engaging with financial markets often involves networking with professionals and peers who have experience in finance. This network can provide mentorship and advice on managing debts, offering practical insights and support that can make debt management more efficient. Economic Awareness A broader awareness of economic conditions and market trends can help individuals anticipate and prepare for changes that might impact their debt management strategies. For instance, understanding economic cycles can inform decisions about when to refinance loans or make extra payments towards debt. Starting to learn about financial markets in youth empowers individuals with the knowledge and tools needed to manage student loans and other debts effectively. This proactive approach can lead to better financial decisions, reduced debt burdens, and a more secure financial future. Creating a Personal Budget and Financial Plan Starting to learn about financial markets in your youth (30s to early 50s) is a crucial step towards creating a personal budget and financial plan for several reasons: Building a Strong Financial Foundation Understanding financial markets helps you grasp key concepts like saving, investing, and managing debt. This knowledge forms the backbone of a strong financial foundation, allowing you to make informed decisions about your money. Long-term Investment Growth Starting early allows more time for your investments to grow. The power of compound interest means that the earlier you start investing, the more you can benefit from exponential growth over time. This is crucial for long-term financial goals like retirement.

Risk Management Learning about financial markets helps you understand the risks involved in different types of investments. This knowledge is essential for creating a balanced portfolio that aligns with your risk tolerance and financial goals. **Financial Discipline** Engaging with financial markets requires a degree of discipline and consistency. This discipline often translates into better personal financial habits, such as regular saving and mindful spending, which are essential components of a solid personal budget. **Economic Awareness** Understanding financial markets keeps you informed about the broader economy. This awareness can influence your personal financial decisions, such as when to buy a house, change jobs, or make significant investments. **Goal Setting** Knowledge of financial markets helps you set realistic financial goals. Whether it's saving for a home, funding your children's education, or planning for retirement, understanding the markets can guide your planning and help you set achievable milestones. **Adapting to Life Changes** Life changes such as marriage, having children, or changing careers impact your financial situation. With a solid understanding of financial markets, you can adapt your financial plan to accommodate these changes, ensuring stability and growth. **Avoiding Financial Pitfalls** Education in financial markets helps you recognize and avoid common financial pitfalls, such as falling into high-interest debt or making uninformed investment choices. This knowledge protects your financial health and promotes sustainable growth. **Maximising Earnings** Learning about financial markets can lead to better career and investment opportunities. Understanding how different industries perform can help you make strategic career moves or invest in promising sectors, maximising your earning potential. **Retirement Planning** Starting early gives you a head start on retirement planning. Understanding financial markets allows you to choose appropriate retirement accounts, such as 401(k)s or IRAs, and make informed decisions about contributions and investments secure your future. In summary, learning about financial markets in your youth sets the stage for creating a comprehensive personal budget and financial plan. It equips you with the knowledge and skills needed to make informed financial decisions, manage risks, and achieve long-term financial stability and growth.

booksasasubject.store

Investing in Higher Education and Skill Development Starting to learn about financial markets in youth (30s to early 50s) can lead to investing in higher education and skill development for several compelling reasons: Increased Financial Literacy Understanding Investment Opportunities Gaining knowledge of financial markets helps individuals recognize the value of investing in education as a long-term investment. Understanding concepts like ROI (Return on Investment) makes it easier to appreciate the benefits of acquiring new skills. informed Decision-Making Financial literacy empowers individuals to make informed decisions about where to allocate their resources. This includes recognizing the potential benefits of higher education and skill development as ways to enhance career prospects and income potential. Enhanced Earning Potential Career Advancement Investing in higher education often leads to better job opportunities and higher salaries. By understanding how the financial markets work, individuals can see education as an investment that pays off through increased earning potential over time. Diversification of Income Streams Learning about financial markets encourages thinking about multiple income streams. Higher education and skill development can open doors to new fields and side projects, providing additional financial security. Long-term Financial Planning Retirement Planning Those who are financially literate understand the importance of long-term financial planning. Higher education can be a crucial part of this plan, ensuring continued employability and income growth as one approaches retirement age. Building Wealth Knowledge of financial markets highlights the importance of continuous personal and professional growth. Investing in education and skills can lead to better job security and career longevity, essential components of wealth building. Adaptability in a Changing Economy Technological Advancements The economy is constantly evolving with technological advancements. Staying updated through continuous education ensures that one remains relevant in their field. Financially savvy individuals understand the necessity of adapting to changes, often facilitated by ongoing learning and skill acquisition. Economic Resilience Understanding financial markets instils a mindset of resilience and preparedness. Investing in education and skills makes individuals more adaptable and better prepared to navigate economic downturns or shifts in the job market.

Increased Confidence and Empowerment Personal Growth Knowledge of financial markets can boost self-confidence. This empowerment often translates into a proactive approach to personal development, including seeking higher education and new skills. Risk Management Learning about financial markets involves understanding and managing risks. This knowledge can be applied to personal development, where individuals learn to take calculated risks in pursuing further education and skill enhancement. Networking and Opportunities Professional Networks Higher education often provides opportunities to build valuable professional networks. Those who understand financial markets know the importance of networking in achieving financial and career goals. Access to Resources Financially literate individuals are better at identifying and accessing resources, including scholarships, grants, and other funding opportunities for further education. Starting to learn about financial markets in one's youth fosters a mindset of growth, informed decision-making, and strategic planning. This naturally extends to recognizing the value of investing in higher education and skill development, leading to enhanced career prospects, better financial stability, and long-term wealth creation. Building Credit: Understanding Credit Scores and Reports Learning about financial markets in your youth, particularly in your 30s to early 50s, can have a direct impact on building credit through several key mechanisms: Understanding Credit Scores and Reports When you engage with financial markets, you inevitably encounter the importance of credit scores and reports. These scores are crucial as they reflect your creditworthiness and are used by lenders to determine your ability to repay debts. By learning early on, you understand how financial decisions impact your credit score. This knowledge allows you to make informed choices, such as paying bills on time, keeping credit card balances low, and managing debt responsibly, all of which are essential for maintaining a healthy credit score. Access to Financial Products As you learn about financial markets, you become aware of the various financial products available, including credit cards, loans, and mortgages. Knowing how these products work helps you choose ones that suit your financial goals and needs. Building a positive credit history early on by using these products responsibly can lead to better terms on future loans and credit lines.

booksasasubject.store

Investment Opportunities Learning about financial markets often goes hand in hand with understanding investment opportunities. As you grow your financial knowledge, you may choose to invest in stocks, bonds, mutual funds, and retirement accounts. Building a good credit score allows you to access favourable interest rates and terms when borrowing to invest, potentially increasing your overall returns. Long-Term Financial Planning Starting young allows you to develop good financial habits and plan for the long term. This includes saving for retirement through vehicles like 401(k)s and IRAs, which often require a solid credit history to access. Understanding financial markets helps you make informed decisions about saving and investing, ensuring you are well-prepared for future financial goals. In summary, learning about financial markets from a young age empowers you to understand credit scores and reports, make wise financial decisions, access beneficial financial products, and plan effectively for your financial future. This foundational knowledge and responsible financial behaviour contribute significantly to building and maintaining a strong credit profile over time.

PEAK ADULT PHASE (50S AND BEYOND)

Wealth Preservation Starting to learn about financial markets during the peak adult phase (50s and beyond) can significantly contribute to wealth preservation for several reasons: Risk Awareness By this stage, individuals have likely accumulated assets and have a clearer understanding of their financial needs, including retirement planning. Understanding financial markets helps in assessing and mitigating risks associated with investments, thereby protecting existing wealth. Long-Term Planning Learning about financial markets allows individuals to make informed decisions about where to allocate their savings and investments. This knowledge helps in choosing diversified portfolios that can weather economic downturns and market volatility, essential for maintaining wealth over the long term. Adaptability The financial landscape evolves continuously, and staying informed about market trends and new investment opportunities is crucial. Starting to learn later in life allows individuals to adapt their financial strategies to changing economic conditions .

and investment climates, thereby preserving and potentially growing their wealth. Estate Planning Wealth preservation also involves planning for the transfer of assets to future generations or beneficiaries. Understanding financial markets helps in making decisions regarding estate planning, taxes, and the most efficient ways to pass on wealth without significant losses.

Avoiding Common Pitfalls Many individuals in their later years may face decisions such as when to draw from retirement accounts, how to manage investments during retirement, and how to protect against inflation. Knowledge of financial markets helps in navigating these decisions wisely, avoiding common pitfalls that can erode wealth. Peace of Mind Finally, knowledge brings confidence. Understanding financial markets empowers individuals to take control of their financial future, reducing anxiety about economic uncertainties and ensuring a more secure financial position for themselves and their families. In essence, starting to learn about financial markets later in life enhances financial literacy, improves decision-making regarding investments and retirement planning, and ultimately contributes to preserving and growing wealth over the long term. Legacy Building Starting to learn about financial markets in the peak adult phase, typically in your 50s and beyond, can significantly contribute to legacy building for several reasons: Accumulated Wisdom and Experience By this stage, individuals have likely accumulated a wealth of life experience and professional expertise. This can translate into a more nuanced understanding of market dynamics, risk management, and long-term financial planning. Focus on Long-Term Goals People in their 50s and beyond are often more focused on long-term financial goals, such as retirement planning, estate planning, and leaving a financial legacy for their heirs. This perspective encourages a strategic approach to investing that aligns with these objectives. Financial Stability Many individuals have reached a more stable financial position in their peak adult phase, having paid off mortgages, funded their children's education, and advanced in their careers. This stability provides a foundation for exploring investment opportunities that can grow wealth over time. Time Horizon for Investments While the time horizon may be shorter compared to younger investors, individuals in their 50s and beyond still have a significant investment horizon ahead, especially considering life expectancy and potential retirement years. This allows for a balanced approach between growth-oriented investments and more conservative strategies to protect accumulated wealth. Impact on Future Generations Learning about financial markets and making informed investment decisions can have a profound impact on future generations. It allows individuals to pass down not just wealth, but also financial literacy and a legacy of responsible financial stewardship.

booksasasubject.store

Adaptability and Resilience Older adults often possess a greater capacity for adaptability and resilience, which are crucial traits in navigating the ups and downs of financial markets. They can leverage their life experiences to make informed decisions and weather market fluctuations more effectively. In essence, starting to learn about financial markets later in life can empower individuals to build a financial legacy by leveraging accumulated wisdom, focusing on long-term goals, and making informed investment decisions that benefit themselves and future generations. Continued Engagement Starting to learn about financial markets in the peak adult phase (50s and beyond) can bring about continued engagement for several reasons: Long-Term Perspective Older adults often have a longer time horizon in mind, such as planning for retirement or managing their wealth through retirement years. This longer-term perspective encourages a deeper understanding of investment strategies and financial planning Personal Relevance As individuals approach retirement age, financial decisions become more critical. Learning about financial markets becomes directly relevant to managing savings, investments, and ensuring financial security for the future. Increased Financial Responsibility With potentially fewer years left in the workforce, there's a heightened awareness of the need to manage finances prudently. This responsibility can motivate older adults to actively engage with financial markets to optimise their savings and investments. Access to Resources Older adults may have more time and resources available for learning compared to earlier stages of life. This can include attending workshops, reading financial literature, or consulting with financial advisors, all of which contribute to continued engagement with financial markets. Adaptability and Lifelong Learning Learning new skills, including financial literacy, contributes to cognitive health and adaptability. Engaging with financial markets fosters a sense of ongoing learning and adaptation to economic changes and market trends. Legacy and Generational Planning Many older adults consider how to leave a financial legacy or plan for future generations. Understanding financial markets allows them to make informed decisions that can impact their families' financial well-being.

Personal Fulfilment Learning about financial markets can be intellectually stimulating and rewarding. It provides opportunities to explore new interests and gain a sense of accomplishment by mastering complex financial concepts. In summary, starting to learn about financial markets in later adulthood encourages continued engagement due to the relevance of financial decisions, increased resources for learning, and the desire to ensure financial security for oneself and future generations. Support for Lifestyle Learning about financial markets and starting to invest later in life, particularly in the peak adult phase (50s and beyond), can bring several benefits that support your lifestyle: Long-Term Financial Security Investing in your 50s allows you to build a nest egg that can provide financial security well into retirement. Even starting later, you still have time to benefit from compounding returns, where your investments generate earnings that are reinvested to generate their own earnings over time. Diversification and Risk Management By diversifying your investments across different assets such as stocks, bonds, and real estate, you can manage risk more effectively. This helps protect your savings from market volatility and economic downturns. Supplementing Retirement Income Investing later in life can supplement other retirement income sources like Social Security or pensions. It provides an additional income stream that can support your desired lifestyle in retirement, covering expenses beyond basic needs. Meeting Healthcare Needs Healthcare costs tend to increase with age. By investing in retirement plans like 401(k)s or IRAs, you can accumulate funds specifically earmarked for potential medical expenses or long-term care needs. Legacy Planning Investing allows you to potentially leave a financial legacy for your loved ones. It can involve building wealth that can be passed onto future generations, supporting their financial goals and aspirations. Lifestyle Flexibility Financial independence gained through investing allows for more flexibility in how you spend your retirement years. Whether it's travelling, pursuing hobbies, or supporting family, having financial resources gives you the freedom to enjoy life on your own terms. Adapting to Inflation Investments in assets that tend to keep pace with or outpace inflation (like stocks) help preserve your purchasing power over the long term. This ensures that your savings maintain their value even as living costs rise.

booksasasubject.store

Professional Advice and Guidance Starting to invest later often means you have more financial resources and possibly access to professional financial advice. This can help you make informed decisions tailored to your specific goals and risk tolerance. While starting to invest earlier in life generally provides more time to benefit from compounding returns, starting in your 50s or later still offers significant advantages in securing your financial future and supporting your desired lifestyle during retirement. Advanced Investment Strategies Starting to learn about financial markets and advanced investment strategies later in life, especially in the peak adult phase (50s and beyond), can bring several advantages: Accumulated Life Experience By the time you reach your 50s and beyond, you likely have a wealth of life experiences and knowledge. This can translate into better decision-making abilities, including understanding risk, patience in investment choices, and a clearer perspective on long-term goals. Stable Financial Situation Many individuals in their 50s have more stable financial situations compared to younger adults. They may have paid off mortgages, have higher salaries, or fewer financial obligations like college tuition for children. This stability can provide a better platform for understanding and managing investments. Longer Investment Horizon Even though you may be closer to retirement, many people in their 50s and 60s still have a significant investment horizon ahead of them, potentially spanning decades. This longer time frame allows for the adoption of more advanced investment strategies that may have higher returns but also come with higher risks. Access to Resources At this stage, individuals often have more financial resources available, which can be allocated towards learning and implementing sophisticated investment strategies. This might include hiring financial advisors, attending specialised courses, or accessing exclusive investment opportunities. Focus on Retirement Planning As retirement nears, there is a heightened focus on retirement planning and ensuring that investments align with long-term financial goals. This can lead to a more disciplined approach to investment strategies and a deeper understanding of retirement vehicles like IRAs and 401(k)s. Adaptability and Learning Capacity Contrary to stereotypes, older adults have shown a capacity for adaptability and learning new skills, including financial literacy and investment knowledge. This adaptability can facilitate the understanding and implementation of complex investment strategies.

Diverse Investment Options With more experience and potentially more disposable income, older adults can explore a broader range of investment options, including alternative investments, international markets, and niche sectors that may require more specialised knowledge. In summary, starting to learn about financial markets and advanced investment strategies later in life can leverage accumulated experience, stable financial situations, and a longer investment horizon. This can lead to more informed decision-making, potentially higher returns, and better alignment with retirement goals. Diversifying Investment Portfolios Learning about financial markets and diversifying investment portfolios in your 50s and beyond can be beneficial for several reasons: Risk Management As you near retirement age, preserving your wealth becomes more crucial. Diversifying your investments across different asset classes (such as stocks, bonds, real estate, etc.) helps spread risk. This means if one sector or asset class underperforms, others may provide stability or growth, reducing overall portfolio volatility. Income Generation Diversification can also enhance your ability to generate income. Different types of investments may produce income streams in various market conditions. For instance, dividend-paying stocks, bonds with regular interest payments, and rental income from real estate can contribute to a steady cash flow, which is important for retirees. Capital Preservation While growth is important, protecting your capital becomes a primary concern in later stages of life. Diversification helps safeguard your savings against major losses that might occur if all your investments were concentrated in a single asset or sector. Diversifying your investments Life circumstances can change unexpectedly, even during retirement. Diversifying your investments ensures you have the flexibility to adjust your financial strategy according to evolving personal needs, economic conditions, and market trends. Long-Term Growth Potential Even in your 50s and beyond, you may have a decade or more of investing ahead. Diversification allows you to capture potential growth opportunities across different sectors and regions. Some investments, like certain stocks or international funds, may offer growth potential that aligns with longer-term retirement goals.

booksasasubject.store

Risk Tolerance and Comfort Older investors often have a lower risk tolerance due to proximity to retirement. Diversification can be tailored to match your risk tolerance and comfort level, ensuring you stay invested in a way that aligns with your financial goals and emotional well-being. In essence, learning about financial markets and diversifying your investment portfolio in later stages of life can help optimise risk and returns, provide income, protect your savings, and adapt to changing circumstances—all crucial factors for securing a comfortable retirement. Real Estate Investment Opportunities Learning about financial markets in your 50s and beyond can indeed lead to real estate investment opportunities for several reasons: Accumulated Knowledge and Experience By your 50s, you likely have accumulated significant life and professional experience. This can include understanding economic cycles, market trends, and potentially having a clearer financial picture regarding savings and retirement plans. This knowledge can help you make informed decisions about real estate investments, which often require a deeper understanding of market dynamics and financial implications. Investment Diversification Real estate offers diversification benefits to your investment portfolio. As you approach retirement, diversifying into assets like real estate can provide stable income streams, potentially hedge against inflation, and offer capital appreciation over the long term. Learning about financial markets can help you assess how real estate fits into your overall investment strategy and retirement planning. Access to Retirement Funds In your 50s and beyond, you may have access to retirement funds such as 401(k)s or IRAs, which can be utilised for real estate investments through methods like self-directed IRAs or specific real estate investment vehicles. Understanding financial markets allows you to explore these options effectively, ensuring you make sound investment choices aligned with your financial goals. Risk Management Real estate investments, like any other asset class, carry risks. Understanding financial markets can help you evaluate these risks more effectively. You can learn to assess property values, rental yields, market demand, and potential risks such as interest rate fluctuations or local economic conditions. This knowledge enables you to make informed decisions and mitigate risks associated with real estate investments.

Networking and Opportunities By engaging with financial markets, you expand your network and potentially gain access to real estate investment opportunities. This can include partnerships with real estate professionals, developers, or access to real estate investment trusts (REITs) and other investment vehicles that specialise in real estate. Networking and staying informed about financial markets can open doors to lucrative real estate ventures that align with your financial goals. In summary, learning about financial markets in your 50s and beyond empowers you to leverage accumulated knowledge and resources effectively. This understanding enables you to identify, evaluate, and capitalise on real estate investment opportunities as part of a diversified and well-managed investment portfolio tailored to your retirement planning needs.

Planning for Major Life Events: Marriage, Children, and Home Buying Learning about financial markets and investing later in life, especially in the peak adult phase (50s and beyond), can still greatly benefit planning for major life events like marriage, children, and home buying for several reasons:

Financial Stability and Security Understanding financial markets helps in building financial stability. This stability is crucial when planning for major life events such as marriage, where combining finances may be necessary, or preparing for the financial responsibilities that come with children or home buying.

Long-Term Planning By learning about financial markets later in life, individuals can better plan for the long term. This includes saving and investing in retirement plans like 401(k)s and IRAs, which are essential for funding major life events and maintaining financial security in retirement.

Investment Knowledge Knowledge of financial markets allows individuals to make informed investment decisions. This can lead to better growth of savings over time, which is important when considering the costs associated with major life events such as buying a home or funding a child's education.

Adjusting Financial Plans In the 50s and beyond, individuals may need to adjust their financial plans to meet changing life circumstances. Understanding financial markets helps in making these adjustments effectively, whether it's reallocating investments, planning for estate management, or optimising retirement income streams.

Risk Management With age comes a need for more conservative financial strategies to protect savings and investments. Learning about financial markets helps in understanding risk management techniques and choosing appropriate investment vehicles that align with personal risk tolerance and financial goals.

booksasasubject.store

Legacy Planning Later in life, individuals often consider legacy planning, including estate planning and charitable giving. Knowledge of financial markets is crucial here for maximising the impact of assets and ensuring financial security for future generations. Overall, starting to learn about financial markets in later adulthood provides the knowledge and tools necessary to plan effectively for major life events, ensuring financial security, stability, and preparedness throughout different stages of life. Preparing for Retirement: Maximising Retirement Savings and Pensions Learning about financial markets and starting to invest in retirement savings later in life, particularly in the peak adult phase (50s and beyond), can still be highly beneficial for preparing for retirement and maximising savings and pensions. Here are several reasons why: Time Horizon and Stability By your 50s, you likely have a clearer picture of your retirement timeline and financial needs. This clarity allows you to make more informed decisions about how much to save and invest to meet your retirement goals. Higher Income Potential Many individuals in their 50s are at their peak earning potential. This can provide the opportunity to save more aggressively towards retirement, taking advantage of higher income levels to contribute more to retirement accounts like 401(k)s or IRAs Catch-Up Contributions The tax code allows for catch-up contributions to retirement accounts for individuals aged 50 and older. For example, in 2024, those over 50 can contribute an extra $6,500 to their 401(k) and an additional $1,000 to their IRA beyond the standard contribution limits. This helps accelerate retirement savings in the later years. Financial Knowledge and Experience With age often comes increased financial literacy and experience. This can translate into more confident and informed decision-making when it comes to investing in financial markets. Older adults may have a better understanding of risk management and asset allocation, which are crucial for optimising retirement portfolios. Diversification and Asset Allocation At this stage, you can focus on diversifying your investments across different asset classes to manage risk and maximise returns. This approach helps in creating a balanced portfolio that is suited to your risk tolerance and retirement timeline.

Planning for Healthcare Costs As you approach retirement age, healthcare costs become a more significant consideration. Learning about financial markets can help you plan for these expenses, whether through dedicated health savings accounts (HSAs) or understanding how Medicare and other insurance options fit into your retirement budget. Long-Term Financial Security Investing in financial markets in your 50s and beyond isn't just about immediate gains; it's about securing your financial future for the long term. Properly managed investments can provide ongoing income during retirement, helping to maintain your lifestyle and cover expenses without relying solely on fixed pensions or Social Security. In essence, starting to learn about financial markets and investing later in life empowers you to make strategic decisions that maximise your retirement savings and pensions. It allows you to leverage your financial experience, income potential, and the benefits of retirement-focused investment strategies to build a stable financial foundation for your retirement years.

THE BENEFITS OF EARLY FINANCIAL INVOLVEMENT

Achieving Financial Independence Early involvement in financial markets can significantly enhance your journey towards achieving financial independence. Here are several key benefits: Compound Interest Early Start The sooner you start investing, the more time your investments have to grow. Compound interest means that you earn returns not only on your initial investment but also on the returns that investment has already generated. Exponential Growth Over time, even small contributions can grow substantially. For example, starting to invest $200 per month at age 25 can result in a much larger nest egg by retirement compared to starting the same investment at age 35 Risk Management Higher Risk Tolerance Younger investors can typically afford to take more risks since they have more time to recover from potential losses. This can allow for a higher allocation in stocks, which historically offer higher returns compared to more conservative investments like bonds. Learning Curve Early involvement allows you to learn and understand market behaviours, risk management strategies, and your own risk tolerance, which can make you a more savvy investor over time. Dollar-Cost Averaging Consistency Investing a fixed amount regularly (e.g., monthly) can help smooth out market volatility. When prices are high, your fixed amount buys fewer shares, and when prices are low, it buys more shares. Reduced Emotional Impact Regular investing can help reduce the emotional impact of market fluctuations, encouraging a long-term perspective rather than reacting to short-term market movements. Financial Discipline and Budgeting Savings Habit Early investment encourages disciplined saving and budgeting habits. Allocating money towards investments rather than spending can lead to better financial management overall. Goal Setting Setting investment goals can help prioritise financial decisions and create a clear path towards achieving financial independence.

Tax Advantages Tax-Deferred Growth Accounts like 401(k)s and IRAs offer tax advantages. Contributions to traditional IRAs and 401(k)s are often tax-deductible, and the investments grow tax-deferred, meaning you don't pay taxes on the earnings until you withdraw the money. Roth Options Roth IRAs and Roth 401(k)s allow for tax-free withdrawals in retirement, provided certain conditions are met. Starting early means more time for your investments to grow tax-free. Time to Correct Mistakes Recovery Time Starting early gives you the opportunity to make mistakes and learn from them without jeopardising your financial future. There's more time to adjust your strategy and recover from any setbacks. Experience and Knowledge Early experience in the markets can help you become a more knowledgeable and confident investor, which is invaluable for long-term financial planning. Greater Financial Flexibility More Options With a larger portfolio built over time, you have more financial options available to you. This could mean retiring earlier, pursuing different career opportunities, or having the flexibility to handle financial emergencies. Wealth Accumulation Early investment can lead to substantial wealth accumulation over time, providing financial security and independence. Beating Inflation Maintaining Purchasing Power Investing in assets that have the potential to outpace inflation helps ensure that your money retains its value over time. Cash savings lose value due to inflation, whereas investments in stocks, real estate, and other assets typically grow at a rate that surpasses inflation. Diversification Portfolio Building Starting early allows you to build a diversified portfolio, spreading your investments across different asset classes to reduce risk. Long-Term Strategy A diversified approach from an early stage can help in achieving a balanced risk-reward ratio, aligning with your long-term financial goals. Starting early in financial markets is one of the most powerful steps you can take towards achieving financial independence. It leverages the benefits of compound interest, allows for greater risk tolerance, encourages disciplined saving, and provides more time to grow your investments. By taking advantage of these benefits, you can build a solid financial foundation that supports your long-term goals and financial security.

Enhancing Decision-Making Skills Early involvement in financial markets can significantly enhance decision-making skills through various mechanisms. Here's a detailed look at how this happens: Increased Financial Literacy Engaging with financial markets necessitates understanding a range of financial concepts such as stocks, bonds, mutual funds, market indices, economic indicators, and financial statements. This foundational knowledge improves overall financial literacy, which is crucial for making informed decisions not just in investments, but in broader financial planning. Risk Assessment and Management Investing early teaches you to evaluate the risks associated with different types of investments. By understanding risk, you become more adept at assessing and managing it, which is a critical skill in all aspects of life, from personal to professional decisions. Analytical Skills Analysing market trends, company performance, and economic conditions requires critical thinking and analytical skills. Over time, regularly making these analyses sharpens your ability to evaluate complex information and make well-informed decisions based on data and trends. Emotional Discipline Financial markets are often volatile, and being involved in them helps you develop emotional discipline. Learning to manage emotions like fear and greed can prevent impulsive decisions and foster a more rational approach to decision-making under pressure, which is valuable in many areas of life. Long-term Planning and Patience Investing early helps you appreciate the benefits of long-term planning and patience. Understanding the power of compounding and the importance of staying invested through market cycles cultivates a mindset that is beneficial for making other long-term life decisions. Continuous Learning Financial markets are dynamic, requiring ongoing education and adaptation to new information. This habit of continuous learning and staying updated with new developments fosters a proactive approach to decision-making and problem-solving. Diversification and Strategic Thinking Investing teaches you the importance of diversification to manage risk and maximise returns. This strategic thinking can be applied to various decision-making processes, where considering multiple options and their potential outcomes leads to more robust and well-rounded decisions. Understanding Economic Impact Early involvement in financial markets provides insights into how global and local economic events impact investments. This understanding can enhance your ability to anticipate and react to economic changes, improving your decision-making in both personal finance and business contexts.

Networking and Resource Utilisation Being involved in financial markets often means interacting with financial advisors, reading financial news, and joining investment communities. This networking helps you learn from others, access diverse perspectives, and utilise resources more effectively, leading to better-informed decisions. Building Confidence Making investment decisions and seeing the outcomes—whether positive or negative—builds confidence in your ability to evaluate options and make choices. This confidence translates into other areas of life, encouraging a proactive and decisive approach to challenges. By cultivating these skills through early involvement in financial markets, individuals can enhance their overall decision-making capabilities, leading to better outcomes in various aspects of their personal and professional lives. Stress Reduction and Financial Security Early involvement in financial markets can significantly reduce stress and enhance financial security through a variety of mechanisms. Here's an elaboration on how this works: Stress Reduction Financial Literacy and Confidence Education and Understanding Early involvement leads to better financial literacy, which means understanding how markets work, knowing the risks and benefits of different investments, and making informed decisions. Confidence As knowledge increases, so does confidence in handling finances, reducing anxiety associated with financial uncertainty. Long-Term Planning Clarity and Control Early planning and investment create a sense of control over financial future, reducing stress related to unpredictability. Goal Setting Establishing clear financial goals (retirement, buying a house, etc.) and working towards them from an early age provides a roadmap, which can be calming. Risk Management Time to Recover Younger investors have more time to recover from market downturns, which reduces the stress of short-term losses. Diversification Starting early allows for gradual and strategic diversification of investments, spreading risk and reducing the impact of any single investment loss.

Financial Security Compound Interest Growth Over Time Investments have more time to grow due to compound interest, significantly increasing wealth over the long term. For instance, even small regular investments can grow substantially over decades. Power of Compounding The earlier you start, the more you benefit from the exponential growth of your investments. Retirement Savings Ample Retirement Funds Early investment in retirement plans (401(k), IRA) ensures a larger nest egg due to prolonged growth periods. Employer Matches Many retirement plans offer employer matching contributions, which is essentially free money contributing to financial security. Emergency Fund Safety Net Investing from an early age helps build an emergency fund, providing a financial cushion in case of unexpected expenses or job loss. Reduced Debt Having savings and investments reduces the need to rely on high-interest debt for emergencies. Wealth Accumulation Asset Building Early and consistent investments build substantial assets over time, which can be used for various financial goals (education, home purchase, etc.). Intergenerational Wealth Accumulated wealth can be passed onto future generations, ensuring financial security for your family. Financial Independence Freedom of Choice With sufficient investments and savings, you gain the freedom to make life choices without being constrained by financial limitations. Early Retirement Building a strong financial foundation early can provide the option for early retirement, if desired. Starting early with financial market investments reduces stress by providing a sense of control, confidence, and security. It also ensures financial security through the power of compound interest, strategic risk management, and accumulation of assets. These benefits contribute to a more stable and less stressful financial future.

Creating Wealth and Generational Financial Health Getting involved in financial markets early offers numerous benefits that can contribute to creating wealth and ensuring generational financial health. Here's an in-depth look at these advantages: Compounding Returns Definition Compounding occurs when the earnings on your investments generate their own earnings over time. Example If you invest $1,000 at a 7% annual return, in 10 years, it will grow to approximately $1,967, and in 30 years, it will be about $7,612. The earlier you start, the more you benefit from compounding. Time to Weather Market Volatility Risk Management Longer investment horizons allow you to ride out market downturns and benefit from the market's overall upward trajectory. Example Historically, the stock market has always recovered from downturns given enough time. Early investments can recover and grow even after temporary losses. Learning and Experience Financial Literacy Starting early gives you more time to learn about financial markets, investment strategies, and risk management. Confidence Building Early experiences, even mistakes, help you become a more knowledgeable and confident investor. Increased Savings Habit Formation Starting early helps inculcate a habit of saving and investing regularly. Higher Contributions Over time, even small, consistent contributions can grow significantly, thanks to the power of regular investing. Tax Advantages Retirement Accounts Investing in retirement accounts like 401(k)s and IRAs can offer tax benefits, such as tax-deferred growth or tax-free withdrawals in retirement. Tax-Efficient Investments Long-term capital gains are typically taxed at a lower rate than short-term gains, providing an additional advantage for early investors.

Financial Security and Independence Emergency Fund Early investment can help build a financial cushion for emergencies, reducing the need to rely on high-interest debt. Retirement Planning Starting early ensures you have enough time to build a substantial retirement fund, reducing stress and providing financial security in later years. Intergenerational Wealth Transfer Estate Planning Early and consistent investing can lead to significant wealth accumulation, which can be passed down to future generations. Education and Opportunities With more wealth, you can provide better education and opportunities for your descendants, creating a cycle of financial stability and growth. Diversification Benefits Asset Allocation Starting early allows you to experiment with different asset classes (stocks, bonds, real estate) and find a mix that works for you. Risk Mitigation Diversifying your investments reduces risk and increases the chances of steady growth over time. Inflation Hedge Real Returns Investments, particularly in equities and real estate, typically outpace inflation, ensuring that your purchasing power grows over time. Wealth Preservation By beating inflation, you preserve and enhance your wealth, safeguarding it for future generations. Early involvement in financial markets provides a solid foundation for creating wealth and ensuring generational financial health. It harnesses the power of compounding, offers learning opportunities, and provides tax advantages and diversification benefits. These factors collectively contribute to financial security, independence, and the ability to transfer wealth to future generations, promoting long-term prosperity.

CASE STUDIES AND REAL - LIFE EXAMPLES

Successful Early Investors Successful early investors often leverage their understanding of financial markets to build substantial wealth over time. Here are some case studies and real-life examples illustrating how early involvement in financial markets can lead to success: Warren Buffett Background Warren Buffett is one of the most successful investors of all time, often referred to as the "Oracle of Omaha." Early Investment Buffett started investing at the age of 11. He purchased three shares of Cities Service Preferred at $38 per share. The stock fell to $27 but later rebounded to $40. He sold it, but the stock eventually went up to $200. Lesson Patience and long-term vision are key. Buffett's philosophy of value investing, which involves buying undervalued stocks and holding them for the long term, has made him one of the wealthiest individuals in the world. Peter Lynch Background Peter Lynch is a famous mutual fund manager who managed the Magellan Fund at Fidelity Investments. Early Career Lynch started his career as an intern at Fidelity while still in college. He began managing the Magellan Fund in 1977. Success Under his management, the Magellan Fund's assets grew from $18 million to $14 billion. He consistently achieved an average annual return of 29.2% over 13 years. Lesson Knowledge and diligent research can lead to remarkable investment success. Lynch believed in "investing in what you know," which helped him identify promising stocks early. Chris Sacca Background Chris Sacca is a venture investor known for his early investments in tech companies like Twitter, Uber, and Instagram. Early Investment Sacca began investing in tech startups during the early 2000s. He purchased shares of Twitter when the company was still a startup.

Success Sacca's early investments in Twitter and other tech giants have made him a billionaire. His firm, Lowercase Capital, became one of the most successful venture capital funds. Lesson Identifying and investing in innovative startups can lead to significant returns. Sacca's ability to recognize the potential in emerging technologies was crucial to his success. . T. Rowe Price Background T. Rowe Price is the founder of the investment firm T. Rowe Price Associates. Early Career Price began his investment career in the 1920s. He founded his firm in 1937, focusing on growth investing. Success Price's emphasis on growth stocks led to the success of his firm, which now manages over $1 trillion in assets. Lesson Growth investing, which involves identifying companies with strong potential for earnings growth, can be a successful strategy. Price's firm has consistently delivered strong returns for its investors. Early Employees of Tech Giants Background Many early employees of companies like Google, Facebook, and Amazon received stock options as part of their compensation. Success Early employees who held onto their stock options have seen substantial wealth accumulation. For example, early Google employees like Susan Wojcicki and Marissa Mayer became multimillionaires due to their stock holdings. Lesson Joining a promising startup and receiving equity can lead to significant financial rewards. Holding onto stock options and believing in the company's long-term success is crucial. Key Takeaways Start Early The earlier you start investing, the more time you have for your investments to grow through compounding. Research and Knowledge Thorough research and understanding of the market can help in identifying undervalued stocks or promising startups.

Long-Term Vision Successful investors often focus on long-term gains rather than short-term fluctuations. Patience and perseverance are essential. Diversification Diversifying your investments can reduce risk and increase the potential for returns. Innovation and Trends Staying ahead of market trends and investing in innovative sectors can yield significant returns. By studying these examples and applying their lessons, you can develop a successful investment strategy and potentially achieve financial success in the long run. Lessons from Financial Failures and Recoveries Certainly! Here are several case studies and real-life examples that illustrate the lessons from financial failures and recoveries in the financial markets: The Dot-Com Bubble (Late 1990s - Early 2000s) Overview The late 1990s saw a massive surge in the value of internet-based companies, leading to a speculative bubble. Many companies with little or no profit were valued at billions of dollars. When the bubble burst in 2000, it wiped out nearly $5 trillion in market value. Lesson Speculation vs. Fundamentals Investors should be wary of speculative investments and focus on the fundamental value of companies. Diversification Avoid putting all investments in one sector. Diversifying across sectors can mitigate risk. Due Diligence Perform thorough research before investing in new or emerging markets. 2008 Financial Crisis Overview The 2008 financial crisis was triggered by the collapse of the housing market in the United States, driven by high-risk mortgage lending and the securitization of these mortgages into mortgage-backed securities (MBS). Major financial institutions faced insolvency, leading to a global economic downturn. Lessons Risk Management Financial institutions need robust risk management practices to avoid exposure to high-risk assets. Regulatory Oversight Strong regulatory frameworks are crucial to monitor and control financial practices.

Transparency Greater transparency in financial products can help prevent systemic risks. Enron Scandal (2001) Overview Enron, once one of the largest energy companies, filed for bankruptcy after it was revealed that it had used accounting loopholes and special purpose entities to hide billions in debt. This scandal led to the dissolution of Arthur Andersen, one of the five largest audit and accountancy partnerships in the world. Lessons Corporate Governance Strong corporate governance and ethical practices are vital for long-term business sustainability. Accountability Ensuring accountability at all levels of management helps prevent fraud and unethical behaviour. Regulation Regulatory bodies must have the power and resources to enforce compliance and transparency. Long-Term Capital Management (LTCM) (1998) Overview LTCM, a hedge fund, used highly leveraged positions in fixed income arbitrage. When the Russian government defaulted on its debt, LTCM's positions led to massive losses, threatening the stability of financial markets. Lessons Leverage Excessive leverage can lead to significant risks and potential financial instability. Liquidity Ensuring liquidity is crucial for managing positions and avoiding forced sales at unfavourable prices. Interconnectedness The interconnectedness of financial institutions can amplify risks and necessitate coordinated responses. Greece Debt Crisis (2010s) Overview Greece faced a severe debt crisis due to high levels of public debt and budget deficits. The crisis led to austerity measures, bailouts from the European Union and the International Monetary Fund, and significant economic and social impacts. Lessons Fiscal Responsibility Maintaining fiscal discipline is crucial for national economic stability. International Cooperation Addressing financial crises may require coordinated international support and intervention.

Structural Reforms Implementing structural reforms can help improve economic resilience and long-term growth prospects. COVID-19 Pandemic (2020) Overview economic disruptions, leading to massive sell-offs in financial markets, government stimulus measures, and central bank interventions to stabilise economies.The global pandemic caused unprecedented Lesson Crisis Management Rapid and coordinated responses are essential in managing economic crises. Adaptability Businesses and economies must adapt to changing circumstances to survive and thrive. Support Mechanisms Strong social and economic support mechanisms can help mitigate the impact of crises on vulnerable populations. These case studies highlight the importance of sound financial practices, regulatory oversight, risk management, and the need for diversification and thorough research. By learning from past failures and recoveries, investors and policymakers can make more informed decisions to build a more resilient and stable financial system. Stories of Financial Growth Across Different Life Stages Exploring case studies and real-life examples of financial growth through the financial markets can be quite insightful. Here are some detailed examples across different life stages: Early Career: Starting Out Case Study: Emma's Roth IRA Journey Background Emma is a recent college graduate who has just started her first job. She's 22 years old, earning $45,000 annually. Financial Strategy Contributions Emma decides to contribute $500 per month to a Roth IRA, maxing out her annual contribution limit of $6,000. Investment Choice She chooses a diversified portfolio of low-cost index funds. Outcome Initial Years In the first few years, Emma sees modest gains as she consistently invests in the market. Compounding Growth After 10 years, her contributions of $60,000 grow to approximately $100,000, assuming an average annual return of 7%.

Long-Term Perspective By the time Emma is 60, her Roth IRA could grow to over $1 million, illustrating the power of starting early and the benefits of compound interest. Mid-Career: Building Wealth Case Study: John and Lisa's 401(k) Strategy Background John and Lisa are a married couple in their early 40s. John earns $80,000 annually, and Lisa earns $70,000. They have been contributing to their 401(k) plans since their late 20s. Financial Strategy Maximising Contributions They both decide to maximise their 401(k) contributions, taking advantage of employer matches. Diversification They allocate their investments across a mix of domestic and international stocks, bonds, and real estate funds. Outcome Steady Growth Over the years, their combined 401(k) balances have grown to $500,000. Market Fluctuations They experience market ups and downs, but their diversified portfolio helps mitigate risks. Future Security By the time they retire at 65, their 401(k) balances could reach $1.5 million, providing comfortable retirement. Pre-Retirement: Transitioning to Retirement Case Study: Maria's Investment Portfolio Adjustment Background Maria is 55 years old and plans to retire at 65. She has saved diligently in her 401(k) and IRA, accumulating $700,000. Financial Strategy Reallocation Maria decides to shift her portfolio to a more conservative mix, focusing on bonds, dividend-paying stocks, and other low-risk investments. Catch-Up Contributions She takes advantage of catch-up contributions, adding an extra $6,500 annually to her 401(k). Outcome Risk Management Her portfolio is less volatile, protecting her savings from major market downturns. Steady Growth With an average annual return of 5%, her portfolio grows to $1 million by the time she retires.

Retirement Income Maria's investments provide a steady income stream, supplemented by Social Security. Retirement: Managing Wealth Case Study: George's Retirement Income Plan Background George is 70 years old and has retired with a $1.2 million retirement portfolio. He aims to maintain his lifestyle without depleting his savings. Financial Strategy Withdrawal Strategy George follows the 4% rule, withdrawing $48,000 annually from his portfolio. Income Sources He diversifies his income sources, including Social Security, dividends, and rental income from a property he owns. Outcome Sustainable Income George's diversified income sources help maintain his lifestyle without relying solely on his retirement savings. Portfolio Longevity With prudent withdrawals and continued investment growth, his portfolio remains robust, ensuring financial stability throughout his retirement. Real-Life Example: Warren Buffett's Long-Term Investment Approach Background Warren Buffett, one of the most successful investors, began investing at a young age and is known for his long-term investment strategy. Financial Strategy Value Investing Buffett focuses on buying undervalued companies with strong fundamentals. Patience and Discipline He holds investments for the long term, allowing compound interest to work in his favour. Outcome Substantial Growth Buffett's net worth has grown to billions, largely due to his disciplined and patient investment approach. Legacy His investment philosophy and success stories continue to inspire individual and institutional investors worldwide. These case studies highlight the importance of starting early, maintaining a diversified portfolio, adjusting strategies based on life stages, and focusing on long-term growth. By following these principles, individuals can achieve financial growth and stability through the financial markets.

CONCLUSION

Recap of Key Points Here is a detailed conclusion on the topic of financial markets and key points to recap: Conclusion on Financial Market Involvement Engaging in financial markets can be a powerful way to build wealth and secure your financial future. However, it requires a solid understanding of the markets, investment strategies, and risk management. The key to successful investing lies in continuous education, strategic planning, and maintaining a disciplined approach. By leveraging various investment vehicles like stocks, bonds, mutual funds, and retirement plans such as 401(k)s and IRAs, investors can create a diversified portfolio that aligns with their financial goals and risk tolerance. Recap of Key Points Understanding Financial Markets Definition Financial markets refer to marketplaces where securities, commodities, derivatives, and other financial instruments are traded. Types of Markets Includes stock markets, bond markets, commodity markets, and foreign exchange markets. Role in the Economy Facilitate the raising of capital, transfer of risk, and international trade. Investment Vehicles Stocks Represent ownership in a company; potential for high returns but come with higher risk. Bonds Debt securities issued by entities; generally lower risk with fixed interest returns. Mutual Funds and ETFs Pooled investment funds that offer diversification and professional management. Real Estate Investing in property can provide rental income and potential appreciation. Retirement Plans 401(k) Employer-sponsored plan allowing pre-tax contributions; often includes employer match. IRA (Individual Retirement Account) Personal retirement plan with tax advantages; includes Traditional and Roth IRAs. Benefits Tax deferral, compound growth, and in some cases, tax-free withdrawals. Investment Strategies Diversification Spreading investments across various asset classes to reduce risk

Asset Allocation Determining the proportion of different assets in a portfolio based on risk tolerance and investment goals. Long-term vs. Short-term Investing Balancing between long-term growth and short-term gains based on financial objectives. Active vs. Passive Management Active involves frequent trading to outperform the market, while passive tracks market indexes. Risk Management Understanding Risk Different types of risk include market risk, credit risk, liquidity risk, and interest rate risk. Risk Tolerance Assessing how much risk you are willing to take based on financial situation and goals. Mitigation Strategies Using diversification, hedging, and insurance to manage and mitigate risks. Importance of Continuous Education Staying Informed Keeping up with market trends, economic indicators, and financial news. Learning Resources Books, courses, financial advisors, and online platforms can provide valuable insights. Adaptability Being flexible and adapting strategies as markets and personal circumstances change. Behavioural Aspects of Investing Emotional Discipline Avoiding impulsive decisions driven by market volatility or hype. Patience and Consistency Staying committed to investment plans and avoiding frequent trading based on short-term market movements. Goal Setting Clearly defining financial goals to guide investment decisions and maintain focus. By understanding and applying these key points, you can navigate financial markets more effectively and make informed investment decisions that align with your financial aspirations.

booksasasubject.store

Resources for Further Education and Involvement Conclusion on Financial Markets Involvement Engaging with financial markets can be a powerful tool for wealth creation, retirement planning, and achieving financial independence. The key to success lies in understanding the fundamentals of various investment options, such as stocks, bonds, mutual funds, ETFs, and retirement accounts like 401(k)s and IRAs. Being aware of market dynamics, economic indicators, and the importance of diversification can help mitigate risks and enhance returns. It's crucial to stay informed, develop a solid investment strategy, and be patient to weather market fluctuations. Starting with a strong financial education, setting clear financial goals, and regularly reviewing and adjusting your portfolio are essential steps in navigating the financial markets effectively. Resources for Further Education and Involvement Books The Intelligent Investor" by Benjamin Graham A classic book on value investing, offering timeless advice on investment strategies. "A Random Walk Down Wall Street" by Burton G. Malkiel Provides insights into various investment strategies and the concept of efficient markets. "Common Sense on Mutual Funds" by John C. Bogle Focuses on mutual funds and the importance of low-cost, diversified investing. Online Courses Coursera's "Introduction to Financial Markets" An overview of financial markets, instruments, and investing principles. edX's "Finance Essentials" Covers the basics of finance, including investment and risk management. Khan Academy's Finance and Capital Markets Free, comprehensive lessons on various financial topics. Websites and Blogs Investopedia A comprehensive resource for definitions, articles, and tutorials on financial concepts. The Motley Fool Offers investment advice, stock picks, and financial news. Seeking Alpha A platform for market analysis and investment research from a community of investors. Financial News Platforms Bloomberg Provides up-to-date financial news, market data, and analysis. CNBC Offers live market updates, investment advice, and expert opinions.

Reuters Finance Delivers global financial news and in-depth market analysis. investment Simulators Investopedia Stock Simulator Allows you to practice trading stocks with virtual money. MarketWatch Virtual Stock Exchange It provides a platform to simulate stock trading and improve your investment strategies. Professional Organizations and Certifications Chartered Financial Analyst (CFA) Institute Offers the CFA certification, a highly regarded credential in investment management. Financial Planning Association (FPA) Provides resources and networking opportunities for financial planning professionals. Certified Financial Planner (CFP) Board Grants the CFP certification, emphasising ethical and competent personal financial planning. Community and Forums Bogleheads Forum A community dedicated to discussing investment strategies inspired by John Bogle's philosophy. Reddit's r/investing A subreddit where users discuss investment strategies, share news, and ask for advice. Morningstar Forums Offers a platform for discussing mutual funds, ETFs, and other investment topics. Financial Advisors Consulting with a certified financial advisor can provide personalized guidance tailored to your financial goals and risk tolerance. By leveraging these resources, you can deepen your understanding of financial markets, enhance your investment skills, and make informed decisions to build a secure financial future. Continuous learning and staying updated with market trends are crucial for successful investing.

THE END ....

WHAT'S NEXT ?

What is next you ask, first of all let me congratulate you for finishing the EBOOK
Now you have successfully absorbed the Financial Market knowledge.

Elephant in the room, of course, what's left of you is to acquire the skill to apply in the Financial Markets and be empowered.

Trading as a Subject Course is a course put together to help you master the Financial Markets and make a career out of it.

NOW GO AHEAD AN DOWNLOAD THE TRADING AS A SUBJECT COURSE ON THE PROVIDED BELOW LINK.

CLICK ON THE LINK BELOW TO CONTINUE ON YOUR VOYAGE.

www.booksasasubject.store

booksasasubject.store

FUN FACTS

Oldest Stock Exchange: The Amsterdam Stock Exchange, established in 1602 by the Dutch East India Company, is considered the world's oldest stock exchange. Ticker Symbols: Ticker symbols for companies on stock exchanges often have interesting origins. For example, Apple Inc.'s ticker symbol "AAPL" reportedly came about because Steve Jobs was a fan of Apple orchards. Bulls and Bears: The terms "bull market" and "bear market" originate from how each animal attacks its opponents. Bulls thrust their horns upwards, symbolising rising prices (optimism), while bears swipe downwards, symbolising falling prices (pessimism). Flash Crash: On May 6, 2010, the Dow Jones Industrial Average plunged nearly 1,000 points in minutes, then recovered. This event, known as the "Flash Crash," was one of the most rapid and severe stock market crashes in history. High-Frequency Trading: Some high-frequency trading firms use algorithms to execute trades in microseconds, faster than the blink of an eye. These firms account for a significant portion of trading volume in major financial markets. Warren Buffett's Office: Despite his immense wealth, Warren Buffett, one of the world's most successful investors, still operates from the same modest office he has used for decades in Omaha, Nebraska. Market Cap: The largest companies by market capitalization often change over time. For instance, in recent years, technology companies like Apple, Amazon, and Microsoft have frequently jostled for the top spot. Black Monday: October 19, 1987, known as Black Monday, saw the largest one-day percentage decline in stock market history, with major indices dropping over 20% in a single day. These facts highlight the rich history and dynamic nature of financial markets, shaped by both economic factors and human behaviour.

BONE OF CONTENTION

A "bone of contention" in financial markets typically refers to a contentious issue or a point of disagreement among investors, analysts, or stakeholders. It often involves topics such as: Valuation: Disagreements over whether a stock, bond, or other asset is overvalued or undervalued. Policy Decisions: Debates regarding central bank policies, government regulations, or fiscal measures that impact markets. Economic Data: Interpretations of economic indicators like GDP growth, unemployment rates, inflation, etc. Corporate Governance: Issues related to how companies are managed, including executive compensation, board decisions, etc. Geopolitical Events: Impact of political instability, trade disputes, or geopolitical tensions on markets. These bones of contention can drive significant volatility and uncertainty in financial markets as participants weigh different perspectives and potential outcomes.

CONCLUSION

The financial markets are complex and dynamic systems where various financial instruments are traded. They play a crucial role in the global economy by facilitating capital allocation, risk management, and price discovery. Key components include: Stock Markets: Where shares of publicly traded companies are bought and sold. Bond Markets: Where debt securities are traded, allowing governments and corporations to borrow funds from investors. Foreign Exchange Markets: Where currencies are traded, facilitating international trade and investment. Commodities Markets: Where raw materials or primary agricultural products are bought and sold. Factors influencing financial markets include economic indicators, geopolitical events, monetary policy decisions, and investor sentiment. Market participants range from individual investors to large institutional investors, each with unique objectives and risk tolerances. Understanding the dynamics of financial markets involves analysing trends, interpreting data, and anticipating changes in economic conditions. Risk management strategies such as diversification and hedging are essential for investors navigating these markets. Overall, financial markets are vital for economic growth and development, but they also carry risks and require careful management and oversight.

booksasasubject.store

RECOMMENDED READING AND RESOURCES

Here's an appendix for understanding financial markets involvement, along with some recommended reading and resources: Appendix: Financial Markets Involvement Understanding Financial Markets: Introduction to Financial Markets Provides an overview of different types of financial markets, including stock markets, bond markets, and derivatives markets. Recommended Reading : "Investing 101: From Stocks and Bonds to ETFs and IPOs, an Essential Primer on Building a Profitable Portfolio" by Michele Cagan. Key Players in Financial Markets Explains the roles of various participants such as investors, issuers, brokers, and regulators. Recommended Reading : "The Intelligent Investor" by Benjamin Graham. Market Instruments and Investment Vehicles Covers different types of financial instruments like stocks, bonds, mutual funds, ETFs, and options. Recommended Reading : "A Random Walk Down Wall Street" by Burton G. Malkiel. Strategies and Approaches: Fundamental Analysis Examines the financial health and performance of companies to determine their investment potential. Recommended Reading : "Security Analysis" by Benjamin Graham and David Dodd. Technical Analysis Focuses on past market data and price trends to forecast future price movements. Recommended Reading , "Technical Analysis of the Financial Markets" by John J. Murphy. Risk Management and Diversification Strategies to manage risk and optimise returns through diversifying investments. Recommended Reading : "The Intelligent Asset Allocator" by William J. Bernstein.

RECOMMENDED READING AND RESOURCES

Resources Online Platforms and Tools Websites like Investopedia, Yahoo Finance, and Bloomberg offer comprehensive financial news, analysis, and tools for investors. Recommended Websites: [Investopedia](https://www.investopedia.com/) [Yahoo Finance](https://finance.yahoo.com/) [Bloomberg](https://www.bloomberg.com/) Financial News and Publications Stay updated with financial news and insights from reputable publications and news channels. Recommended Publications : The Wall Street Journal, Financial Times, and Forbes. Courses and Webinars Online courses and webinars can provide structured learning on various aspects of financial markets. Recommended Platforms : Coursera, edX, and Khan Academy offer courses on finance and investing. Conclusion Understanding financial markets involves continuous learning and staying updated with market trends and investment strategies. Utilise these resources to build a solid foundation and enhance your knowledge in financial markets involvement.

FINANCIAL PLANNING TOOLS AND TEMPLATES

When discussing financial markets involvement within the context of financial planning tools and templates, it typically involves several key components and considerations. Budgeting Tools Tools and templates that help individuals or organisations create and maintain budgets. These can range from simple spreadsheets to more sophisticated software that categorises expenses, tracks income, and forecasts future financial situations. Investment Calculators These tools help in estimating potential returns on investments, analysing different investment options, and understanding the impact of factors like inflation and taxes on investment growth. Retirement Planning Tools Often includes calculators that project retirement savings needs based on current savings rates, expected retirement age, and desired retirement income. They can also help optimise contributions to retirement accounts like 401(k)s and IRAs. Risk Assessment Tools Tools that evaluate an individual's risk tolerance and suggest appropriate investment strategies based on risk profiles. This can include questionnaires and simulations to gauge reactions to market volatility. Asset Allocation Models Templates that recommend how to distribute investments across different asset classes (stocks, bonds, cash equivalents) based on factors like risk tolerance, investment goals, and time horizon. Tax Planning Calculators These tools help in estimating tax liabilities based on income, deductions, and investments. They can also suggest strategies to minimise tax burdens through methods like tax-loss harvesting or retirement account contributions. Estate Planning Templates Tools that assist in organising and planning the distribution of assets after death, including wills, trusts, and beneficiary designations. Financial Goal Trackers Templates that allow users to set financial goals (such as saving for a house or college education) and track progress toward those goals over time. Debt Management Tools Tools that help in managing and paying of debts efficiently, including debt payoff calculators and strategies for debt consolidation or restructuring. Educational Resources Access to information and guides on financial planning topics, including articles, videos, and workshops to educate individuals on financial markets, investment strategies, and personal finance management. These tools and templates are designed to empower individuals to make informed financial decisions, manage risk, and achieve their financial goals effectively within the framework of engaging with financial markets.75

REFERENCE

When discussing financial markets involvement within the context of financial planning tools and templates, it typically involves several key components and considerations. Budgeting Tools Tools and templates that help individuals or organisations create and maintain budgets. These can range from simple spreadsheets to more sophisticated software that categorises expenses, tracks income, and forecasts future financial situations. Investment Calculators These tools help in estimating potential returns on investments, analysing different investment options, and understanding the impact of factors like inflation and taxes on investment growth. Retirement Planning Tools Often includes calculators that project retirement savings needs based on current savings rates, expected retirement age, and desired retirement income. They can also help optimise contributions to retirement accounts like 401(k)s and IRAs. Risk Assessment Tools Tools that evaluate an individual's risk tolerance and suggest appropriate investment strategies based on risk profiles. This can include questionnaires and simulations to gauge reactions to market volatility. Asset Allocation Models Templates that recommend how to distribute investments across different asset classes (stocks, bonds, cash equivalents) based on factors like risk tolerance, investment goals, and time horizon. Tax Planning Calculators These tools help in estimating tax liabilities based on income, deductions, and investments. They can also suggest strategies to minimise tax burdens through methods like tax-loss harvesting or retirement account contributions. Estate Planning Templates Tools that assist in organising and planning the distribution of assets after death, including wills, trusts, and beneficiary designations. Financial Goal Trackers Templates that allow users to set financial goals (such as saving for a house or college education) and track progress toward those goals over time. Debt Management Tools Tools that help in managing and paying of debts efficiently, including debt payoff calculators and strategies for debt consolidation or restructuring. Educational Resources Access to information and guides on financial planning topics, including articles, videos, and workshops to educate individuals on financial markets, investment strategies, and personal finance management. These tools and templates are designed to empower individuals to make informed financial decisions, manage risk, and achieve their financial goals effectively within the framework of engaging with financial markets.

ADDITIONAL READING MATERIALS

Learning about financial markets and their involvement in personal finance and investment can be a rewarding journey. Here are some key areas and additional reading materials to consider. Understanding Financial Markets Books "A Random Walk Down Wall Street" by Burton Malkiel, "The Intelligent Investor" by Benjamin Graham, and "Market Wizards" by Jack D. Schwager are classics that cover different aspects of financial markets, investing strategies, and the psychology of trading. Online Resources Investopedia (www.investopedia.com) offers comprehensive articles on financial markets, investment strategies, and market news. Courses Platforms like Coursera and edX offer courses on financial markets and investments from universities like Yale and Wharton. Investment Vehicles Books "The Little Book of Common Sense Investing" by John C. Bogle is excellent for understanding index funds and passive investing. Websites Vanguard (www.vanguard.com) and Fidelity (www.fidelity.com) provide insights into various investment vehicles such as mutual funds, ETFs, and retirement accounts. Journals Journals like the Journal of Finance and the Journal of Financial Economics offer academic insights into financial markets and investment vehicles. Retirement Planning Books "Your Money or Your Life" by Vicki Robin and Joe Dominguez, "Retire Inspired" by Chris Hogan, and "The Bogleheads' Guide to Retirement Planning" by Taylor Larimore provide guidance on retirement planning strategies. Websites The IRS website (www.irs.gov) offers detailed information on retirement accounts like 401(k)s and IRAs, including contribution limits and tax implications. Financial Planners Consulting with a certified financial planner (CFP) can provide personalised advice on retirement planning based on individual financial goals and circumstances.

ADDITIONAL READING MATERIALS

Market Analysis and Research Books "Security Analysis" by Benjamin Graham and David Dodd, "Technical Analysis of the Financial Markets" by John J. Murphy, and "Stocks for the Long Run" by Jeremy J. Siegel delve into market analysis techniques. Websites Bloomberg (www.bloomberg.com) and CNBC (www.cnbc.com) offer market news, analysis, and expert opinions on financial markets globally. Financial Analysis Tools Platforms like Yahoo Finance and Google Finance provide tools for analysing stocks, mutual funds, and market trends. These resources should provide a solid foundation for understanding financial markets, investment strategies, retirement planning, and market analysis. Depending on your specific interests and goals, you can delve deeper into each area with additional reading and research.

INDEX

The "index of financial markets" typically refers to a measure that represents the performance of a group of stocks or other assets in a particular financial market. Some well-known indices include: Dow Jones Industrial Average (DJIA) Tracks 30 large, publicly owned companies in the United States. S&P 500 Represents the performance of 500 large companies listed on stock exchanges in the United States. NASDAQ Composite Measures the performance of more than 3,000 common stocks listed on the NASDAQ stock exchange. FTSE 100 Index of the 100 companies listed on the London Stock Exchange with the highest market capitalization. Nikkei 225 Stock market index for the Tokyo Stock Exchange, representing 225 large companies listed in Japan. DAX Blue chip stock market index consisting of the 40 major German companies trading on the Frankfurt Stock Exchange. These indices provide a snapshot of how the overall market or specific sectors are performing. Each index has its own methodology for calculating and weighting its components based on various factors such as market capitalization, price-weighted average, or other criteria.

www.ingramcontent.com/pod-product-compliance
Lightning Source LLC
Chambersburg PA
CBHW070351230526
45471CB00006B/2516